Touched

By
Tim Uhr

PublishAmerica
Baltimore

ISBN: 1-59129-334-0
PUBLISHED BY PUBLISHAMERICA BOOK
PUBLISHERS
www.publishamerica.com
Baltimore

Printed in the United States of America

Touched
is dedicated to the memories of three great spirits
and one whom I never had the fortune to meet—yet
is still an inspiration in my life today.

Thanks to:

Bonnie for her sparkling eyes and resilient spirit.

Mom, Pat, April, Jean, Marilyn and Mat for caring.

Bob, Carol, Glenn, Tracy and Daryl for being friends.

John, Dad and Tom for always being with me.

Thanks largely to those I've forgotten to include,
for without them I wouldn't be writing *this*.

PART A

GROUNDED

A wounded bird flitters along the side of the road. A man walks up to the mangled bird, it tries to fly, hop, or roll away from the intruder. Its panicked attempts lead nowhere, and soon the bird is in the man's hands. Feathers float to the ground as the man pulls the bird's wing, extending it out straight from the creature's body. The bird stops fighting. The man looks to be cradling the bird to his chest.

This man then raises up his hands and the bird takes off into the sky.

"Must have been only stunned." I mutter to myself as I hurry past, looking at my watch, noting I only have ten minutes to make my appointment.

With a quick glance back to the man, I see that he is already walking off in a different direction.

CHAPTER 1

CLUTCH

"You don't look so happy."

The interruption of my thoughts. Startled back to reality.

Reality is a bar, and a man sitting next to me. A stranger, no...perhaps it is me who is stranger.

I don't know this man, nor do I know happiness.

Happiness, is it too much to ask for?

I've had fleeting glimpses of happiness. But it never lasts. Many things can make me happy; love, a raise, a friend at a time of need, a smile from a stranger that communicates with my soul, a good meal, a good cup of hot chocolate with a warm ski lodge around it, good sex, a sunny day...somehow the list is longer than my happiness.

It is all so artificial. These things come into my life to show me what happiness could be. But when I try to hold on to them they slip through my fingers.

To a tormented soul, happiness is the calm before the storm. But I am one to never see the storm coming. My focus always seems within, making most of my interactions with the outside world surrealistic. It's rare when an outside influence is strong enough to break through my private bubble.

Even now, this man, who is roughly my age, sits next to me at the bar, his attention on me. But as I glance his way it is obvious that he thinks his statement has gone by totally ignored, for he's now a million miles away, staring at his beer.

Was I attracted to this man? Something about him was alarming. His baby blue eyes somehow didn't fit the rest of his appearance. He was a big man, somehow strong without coming across as macho. Maybe it's that I sensed vulnerably from him. His bulk and size, there only to cover the frailties within. I could picture this man falling down in a china shop, but the only thing he would break would be his neck.

This man, who sat next to me, was far from my concept of a "dream man." I have always been more attracted to the scholarly type, the weaklings who sacrifice their outside strength for a greater strength within. Somehow it correlates to a deep-rooted belief I have that men use their physical beings to hide their flawed essences within.

But this man, who no longer focused any of his attention on me, was different. I could feel it. And my first impressions were always right, whether I choose to acknowledge them or not.

Still unsure if I was attracted to this man, I know at least that he was attracted to me. It was a safe assumption. Men are always attracted to physical appearance, and I've often been told that mine is about as close to perfect as it gets. Blond, blue eyes, a figure that stays 35" 24" 34" even when I don't work at it. I have a face that has been on the cover of magazines. I am comfortable with my beauty. It is something I have had to live with my whole life and, truthfully, have only come to honestly accept within the last three years.

I no longer have to hide behind my looks.

When he looked over at me, what did he see? Another pretty girl? But is that all he sees in me? Looks are enough to get men's attention, but do I have enough substance to hold it? Can my inner beauty ever match my outer?

The more I think, the more the fear inside escalates. Thoughts lead to inaction. Who is this man anyway? Just a stranger in a bar. Probably either out for a one-night stand, or to drown in his alcoholism. Why is it so important to get and hold his attention? Maybe he is just a symbol of all the past men in my life who I never let get close enough to see the real me. I have been too afraid to share my true self with any of them. My beauty was definitely skin deep, and I would not let anyone in to see any further.

My symbolic man, sitting at the bar, in the stool next to me. Probably he has long since forgotten I am even here.

On cue, he casts a quick, but revealing, glance my way, and I instantly know that he is not just like one of the many from my past. He is different.

His was a gentle spirit. I felt safe. I felt a warmth coming from him. More than a warmth, I sensed a spark, a fire.

I could feel this man's power. Maybe this man had the key to happiness.

Breaking the silence like a thunderbolt on a clear night, I found myself saying, "I am unhappy at my cluttered thoughts that dampen my spontaneity."

At first I wasn't sure he knew that I was talking to him. Finally, he turned to me as a spring breeze, just his look enough to bring a thaw to my winter ice.

"I admire someone who understands themselves so well."

I didn't know what to say. How do you respond to something like that?

Before I could think of a thing to say he asked, "How come you don't seem satisfied?"

I could tell from the start that this wasn't going to be a normal bar conversation, but I still couldn't tell where he was coming from.

"No, really," I mustered up my most sincere voice, "this drink is mixed very well. I am very satisfied."

"Is that what your heart wanted to say, or is that coming from your head?"

Who did this guy think he was? "O.K. if you don't like my jokes, and you think I'm a walking analytical machine, and you obviously aren't blown away by my looks, why are we sitting here carrying on this...for lack of a better word...conversation?"

"You are obviously very beautiful. You know that. I know that. You want to ask the bartender? I know he would agree."

That was the worst way I have ever been told I am beautiful. I've heard it from thousands of people, hundreds of ways, but never anything close to that!

Before I could fully process that, and come back with a response, he went on, "But I see something more...hidden. And I got to wondering...if you ever let it out?"

Suddenly I found it hard to swallow.

"Your beauty is powerful, but I think you use it to hide something you fear is even more powerful. What is it you hide?"

My eyes, like clouds in the spring. That ominous first drop of rain trickles down my cheek. My head—trying to control the weather and deny the coming storm, while my heart does a rain dance. My fear grows as the thunder rolls over me.

"By being numb to the pain and fear, you also remove yourself from experiencing the joy. Or is it the joy and pleasure you fear most?"

Oh God. Stop it! Stop his talking...stop my tears.

"Fear is most often what keeps us stuck. Fear is natural. It's all right. Facing fear is the only way to move on, to grow."

Crying in a bar. Who is he that he could do this to me? I must control these tears. It is silly.

Then he touched me. In a bar.

This man I do not know, came and put his arm around me. An arm he obviously no longer wanted!

Sure it was a perfectly natural thing; I often let strangers fondle me in bars.

But as he pulled me toward him, I, busy fighting the tears, found it hard to fight him too.

He pulled me close. He didn't grab at me. Holding me, "It's all right," he said.

What's all right!? The fact that I'm so screwed up? The fact that I let this man molest me in a bar...but no, he held me, not in a sexual way. It was comforting, warm. I think it was different from how I have ever been held before. Somehow I couldn't even picture one of his hands moving slyly to one of my tits. But that is what he wanted. Wasn't it? This had to be a trick. Get me comfortable, relaxed, then...attack!

"It's OK," his voice so soothing. "Cry. Let it out."

He's not telling me not to cry? Who wants to take home a hysterical woman? No one wants to be screwing someone who is crying...

Crying. Like a dam breaking loose. I could no longer control it. Sobs welled up from my very soul. I was not conscious of anything I did. I may have cried for hours there in his arms. Safe. Safe from the world, and my own judgements.

He never attempted to quiet me, though I must have embarrassed him so. He actually seemed sincere in encouraging me to get it all out, and God, I had a lot of it in me. Yes, didn't I even hear him saying, "make the noise," when I quivered from the things inside that I so feared letting out?

Not just tears, they were sobs of pain.

When it all finally stopped and I seemed, for the time being, to have no more possible tears inside me, I would have thought that the embarrassment would have been earth shattering. But I didn't leap from his arms, run from the bar, never to look back—or come back, to that unbearable place again.

He stayed there and, more significantly, I stayed there. I even let him continue to hold me.

His hands never did move anywhere threatening. I no longer envisioned his hands moving to my tits. I no longer feared it. I could not even imagine it now.

I looked at him. His eyes, so penetrating, looked into my soul. I did not resist. I let him in. I felt an energy pass through our eyes.

His eyes so beautiful, or were they my eyes? Our eyes were one, for I not only saw him, but through him I saw myself. I saw myself as I have never before dared to look. But it wasn't so bad. So much of the pain was gone. Maybe I did have a sliver of what's called "inner beauty." I knew it could never compete with my "outer beauty," but it was a start.

* * *

It's been over a month since our encounter in the bar. He is not now my lover. We are not friends. I have not seen him since. He has not called. He never asked for my number. I didn't go home with him that night. After my crying fit, we just talked a while longer, and since it had grown late, we said our good-byes with a hug.

"Call me anytime," he said as he gave me his number. He left it at that. No promises. No requests.

I fully expected to run into him again, or to get a surprise call late one night. Surely he would find a way to get my number; track me down.

But not a sign, or a word. I even went back to that same bar a few times, just to see if I would run into him, but he never came back. I even asked the bartender if he had seen him again, but the bartender couldn't even remember him. "Obviously not a regular." The bartender smiled. Neither was I, but the bartender seemed to have no difficulty remembering me.

PART B

SNOW BLIND

There is something wonderful about snow. I have always loved it. As a kid I played in it, and as a skier I prayed for it.

I may be crazy, but there is something magical about being in a snowstorm. Oh, not shut indoors and trapped by one, or even fighting your way down a slippery highway, but to be out in it. Just you and the elements. I love to walk, looking up to be hypnotized by falling snow.

It was one such day, and I was out walking along without a care. For I had come to realize, some time ago, that snow was my insulation. Snow was the barrier between the outside, hurting world and me. It protected me. Whether it was by way of the snowmen I used to build, when I was small, in front of our home, to stand as guards of protection, or as layered snow to glide me safely down from the top of a hill, making me feel one with my skis.

There was safety in snow. Evil did not come out in snowstorms. There was no snow in Hell.

I walked alone. In silence. For no other fool would brave a night like this.

The snow fell in armfuls. Thus, I was startled when I did encounter another soul out in this weather.

I didn't see him at first, but he was identified by a scraping sound that came from ahead.

The snow was falling so hard I was right next to him before I saw him. He stepped aside for me to pass, wordless, breathing hard, shovel in hand.

I gazed before me at a clear sidewalk. I stopped in my tracks, afraid to trample upon his perfect sidewalk.

"Isn't this an exercise in futility?" I couldn't help but ask.

"Why do you say that!?" An exaggerated smile broke from his lips.

"Look at this snow! It's coming down as hard as can be! Your sidewalk will be covered in ten minutes."

"Then I finished just in time for you!"

I stood, unable to move.

He gestured me forward.

Still I stood motionless.

"Please, before it is covered again," he winked.

"Thanks," was all I said as I continued on my journey. But somehow my path ahead seemed to have been changed, forever.

CLUTCH

Life, for the last month, has been a roller coaster ride. My moods change for no particular reason, I feel I can no longer control my emotions. I am worried that at any moment I will burst out crying in the most unusual place.

I do find myself trusting people more, leaving me feeling vulnerable and afraid—which isn't always bad, because I feel people drawing near me like never before when I feel most vulnerable. And I see them as also vulnerable, and somehow that is something I never knew I shared. My fears, when uncloaked and held up to the light, seem natural and not so consuming. I find myself working through my fears. And there is nothing quite as rewarding as facing a fear, seeing it for what it is, only to later be able to laugh at it.

But I'm not always laughing. Often the fears still win; sometimes I have to run. It is so painful to again feel like the little girl who used to run up to her room because there were so many children who wanted to play. I would feel as if I could be used up. If I spread myself too thin there would soon be nothing left of me. So many demands. I ran from choices, hid from decisions. I couldn't be everyone's friend, but I also couldn't live with choosing one over another. I was too young. I felt like I was playing god.

"You're so popular," Mother would say. "Take advantage of it while you can, you may not always have it."

If only I could ever have figured out what "it" was. It was never something I asked to have, yet a part of me feared losing it. Wasn't it always bad to lose something? Though I didn't ask for this "it" that made me popular, what would I be if I lost "it"? I was nervous to have this thing I could not grasp hold of, with my hands or my mind, but it terrified me to think of losing it, and possibly losing me. For what if that's all I was?

My vulnerability is sometimes so overwhelming I'm sure that I will shatter into a million pieces. I feel so broken that if I allow any further cracks I will never be able to be repaired. When will I pass the point of no return?

He did this to me. Simply with a hug, and by being there. His power scared me. Knowing him for those few small hours had changed me. What would it be like to have him in my life from day to day?

I want to change, but a big part of me is comfortable with my past pains. He opened a door for me. And although I often trip on the threshold, I am now at least aware that there is a door. I can enter the new opening any time I choose, and I can choose to also retreat to my safe old space, knowing that the door can open again for me in the future, when I am ready.

I find myself holding a piece of paper up to a light. It has his handwriting on it. His phone number, with the name "Stephen Mioyu" written neatly underneath. His writing is clear, but childish.

The numbers almost seem to dial themselves.

The phone is ringing. I press the receiver almost violently to my ear.

"Hello." It is him.

Unsure of what to say, I wait...

"Hello?" he says a second time, I doubt there will be a third.

"Hi, this is Liz. From the bar. Almost a month ago. Well, actually it was over a month. The crying fool. I borrowed your shoulder. I..."

"How are you?" he asked.

"I am well."

"You don't sound happy."

"Please! I didn't call up to cry."

"Why did you call?"

"Just to see how you are."

"It's twelve-thirty, on a Wednesday. Somehow I find it hard to believe that you called just to talk."

"You do sound tired. Sorry. Did I wake you?"

"Yes."

Damn him! This was too difficult. I didn't know what I wanted him to say—Hell, I didn't know what I wanted to say! But this wasn't going at all like I pictured. I was grasping to get back the closeness I had with him before. It had only lasted an instant, and a month had passed since we had shared that instant, perhaps it was one of those fleeting moments that you can never return to.

"I'm tired," said the voice I longed to hear whispered in my ear. Why couldn't it be saying what I wanted to hear?

The bastard! Couldn't he tell this was hard for me? Where was the warmth I felt from him before?

"I haven't gotten much sleep lately, and tonight I'm trying to catch up. It's been hectic for me lately. Can I give you a call tomorrow?"

I said, "I'll call you again sometime," and hung up.

Feeling like a little girl, I turned on the TV. I ran through the channels a couple of times, and when nothing caught my eye, I turned it off and went to bed.

For the first time in a month I cried. The tears flowed and the sobs came up freely, almost as I had cried with him.

I cried myself to sleep.

I planned to call him the next day, but somehow never got around to it. I was home all evening, and each time I walked by the phone I gave it an accusing look, but it never rang once all night.

Friday came, and I stumbled through my workday. It was the last workday of the week, and while the office was at its usual "Friday's finally here!" state of mind, I found myself rather distant from that feeling.

I had slipped through Thursday numb to everything. Friday I was worse. I felt so alien with my co-workers, whom I usually joined in with on the typical Friday banter.

So what that it was Friday? There would be more Fridays, just as there would be more Mondays. The days and weeks slip by as if I'm on a huge treadmill. I know a large part of me is sleeping as I walk along. It's only frightening those few moments that I come fully awake and am unsure if I am even walking in the right direction. Most times I come to the conclusion that the direction I walk in, either with or against the treadmill, really makes very little difference. The treadmill moves constantly, inevitably, toward the future. To death. We can walk with it, and go as Lemmings to face our future; or we can spend our life running against the inevitable, pretending to make headway, when all we are really doing is buying a little time.

Time is the illusion of lost souls. Pretending to put order in everything that is; time allows us to divide up the pain. It allows us to delay the now. Time falsely divides the past, present, and future into places. We can spend our time living in the past, thinking about the future, or merely counting time.

Time and dates are barriers to keep us from our feelings. By not acknowledging the control over our own feelings, we give our power away to time. Birthdays, holidays, and anniversaries are set points in time we give our emotions to. We expect to feel certain emotions on certain days, and like sheep we wonder how we got led wrong when we find ourselves where we think we should be, but with feelings that don't match the place. I'm supposed to be happy on my birthday, around Christmas and on other certain holidays. Paint on a smile and think about past times when these dates made you happy.

We start off in an attempt to fool the world, trick it into our own reality, until we eventually realize that the world is already our own reality and we have been only fooling ourselves all along.

Pretend. The art of pretending is a skill best used on oneself. The ultimate masturbation.

"Is something wrong, Liz?"

Drifting back to Friday...reality. A co-worker stands above me, concern in his eyes.

I want to tell him of my fear. So many things I want to say...but it is not Stephen.

Joe Merick stands, waiting for a response. He is about as far from Stephen as it gets. He is the office playboy. I may be one of the only girls in the building he hasn't been to bed with. It's not that he hasn't tried, and it's not that he isn't good-looking, it's just he's not my type. The Greek Adonis type that for a night next to that body most girls will sell their souls. Muscles upon muscles, capped off with crystal blue eyes, and dark, wavy hair. His was a sexuality that oozed from his pores, flowed with his speech, and controlled his every move.

"Liz?" A huge hand came down to touch my cheek. His hand was so large, but it was gentle as it brushed my skin.

I sat frozen.

He pulled his hand away in confusion when I still made no response. I wanted to reach for him, let him touch me again. I wanted to feel. I was sick of the numbness.

I looked up to meet his eyes. They darted away. I waited for him to look back at me, but he wasn't able to meet my gaze.

Instead he said, "Some of us are going down to Haley's Pub after work. It will cheer you up. Why don't you come?"

"I'll think about it."

I could sense something switching inside him as he said, "Or we could just go back to my place." He winked at me, and now he had no problem looking directly at me.

It was I, this time, who looked away.

PART C

THOSE WHO WAIT

Waiting in line. A line like a snake, ready to pounce once the ticket window opens. A sold out show the only guarantee. I had come early, to wait in line, long before the box office opened.

Still, there were many others who came earlier. The line ahead of me was long. How early had those in front of me come? Had they waited all night?

I wanted to see the show, but I guess not quite as badly as those ahead of me. I just hoped the tickets wouldn't run out before they got to me.

Then I looked behind. Yes, there were those who had come later than I. So did I want the tickets more than they did? The line behind me was almost as long as that in front of me. Did all these people really expect to get tickets? Or did the people at the back of the line merely enjoy standing in line? Surely they did not seriously think that there would still be tickets available when it came to their turn.

The line moved steadily now, as I inched my way toward the box office window.

Watching each person who had bought tickets as they made their way back past me, I noted the smiles on their faces—wallet lighter, yet they had gotten what they came for. And as each smiling face passed, my fear of the box office running out of tickets before I got to the front of the line grew.

Then came this man. He had bought tickets. I don't know what made my eyes stay on him after he passed, but I watched him go to the end of the line. He tapped the last person in line on the shoulder and asked, "How many tickets were you going to buy?"

When the last person in line said nothing, this man with the tickets explained, "I bought extra..."

"Uh, just two..." finally came the response.

He then asked the person in front of him, and the person in front of them, and he went down the back of the line asking the last ten people or so. Most people told him how many tickets they had planned to purchase, only one said, "I'm not paying you a penny more than they're worth!"

Then this man dug into his pockets, pulling out his tickets. "Must be a scalper." My thoughts were similar to the person who questioned the price.

He handed the top two tickets off his stack to the last person in line. "Here," was all he said.

Then he moved to the next person to last in line, but before he could say anything the last person in line asked him, "How much do I owe you?"

"You also wanted two," said the man to the next person as he handed out two more tickets. He turned back around to address the last person, "Nothing. I don't need them, they're extra."

He went on like this, not accepting a penny, until all his tickets were gone, skipping only the person who had questioned price. "You obviously didn't think the tickets were worth much," he simply said.

Needless to say, there were some very happy people at the end of the line.

I glanced to the front of the line, still a distant hope away, then back again to the rear. Happy people on both sides of me. And I, in the middle, feeling anxious, feeling cheated.

As the line slowly crawled forward, I had a feeling, deep in the pit of my gut that I knew what would happen.

And when it did, I stomped off to see if I could find that man again. Turns out he wasn't far away.

"Do you realize you cheated many other people in line?" I asked him.

"Huh?"

"By buying so many tickets, and giving them away to those at the end of the line, the people in the middle ended up without tickets."

"I paid for the tickets, they were mine to do with as I choose."

"But you didn't even want the tickets! I saw that you kept none for yourself!"

"I did too want the tickets. So that I could give them away."

I argued a bit more with him, but the thing that stayed with me was one of the last things he said, "In some places, those who were last shall be first."

CLUTCH

I fully expected to go straight home after work, but instead I found myself at the bar.

I rarely went to bars with friends or co-workers. I didn't generally drink for the party atmosphere, I drank for relaxation. I usually drank alone.

I surprised myself by being there, but I thought that Joe would be even more surprised. However, he took it in stride.

"Hey, babe, you made it!"

I shot him a look fully expected to destroy.

He went on undaunted, "Let me buy the beautiful lady a drink."

I went to say hello to the rest of the people I knew there, doing my best to ignore Joe.

I had a drink. Then another. Then I wondered why I was counting. But after the second drink I didn't want anymore, yet I wanted to be drunk.

I needed to escape. I didn't know where, and I didn't dare wonder why, but for the moment I could no longer be me.

I would be an actress!

I accepted more drinks but found ways to dispose of them without actually drinking them.

I stumbled on my way to the bathroom. I said things I can only imagine saying when I'm drunk. I unbuttoned the top two buttons of my blouse. I flirted with every guy, except Joe. I had the eye of every guy in the place on me as I stretched, testing the strength of the rest of my buttons on my blouse, and as I continually knocked things on the ground, shamelessly having to bend over to pick them up.

I was putting on a show. I was the center of attention. I pretended I was too far gone to notice, but I took in every bit of it. I finally had my sexuality working for me. I was having fun with my looks, instead of dreading them and the responses they brought. Now I enjoyed the eyes upon me, and the flirtation. I went with the flow.

It was such a game, and everything was going so smoothly, until out of nowhere a voice said, "I think you've had enough."

It was Joe.

"What? Who do you think you are to tell me what to do!?" The actress in me was slipping away.

Placing an arm around me he said, "I just don't want you to do anything foolish, anything you will regret."

"I don't understand, don't you find me sexy anymore?" I licked my lips, in an attempt to bring the actress back.

I could see it was working. He shuffled his feet and stammered, "I've just never seen you like this."

"There are many ways you haven't seen me." With a nod and a quick turn of the hips, I turned from him and headed to the bar.

But Joe came around to front me before I could reach my destination.

"Where are you going?" he asked.

"If there's not a man around to buy a lady a drink, then I'll have to get one myself."

"I thought we agreed you had enough."

"Enough of you maybe..."

Suddenly I felt a hand on my back. With Joe in front of me, stopping my advancement toward the bar, and now this person who had crept up from behind, I felt trapped.

I swung around, knocking his hand away.

I let out a startled gasp. It was Chris Fletcher. From the office. He was quiet, unassuming, and his brain was bigger than his biceps. I liked Chris.

I had imagined countless affairs with this man. I always felt that the feeling was mutual, but neither one of us ever got around to doing anything about it.

What was Chris doing here? I didn't notice when he came in. He wasn't here when I came in, but he may have been here for an hour for all I knew. Chris wasn't one to announce his entrance.

I suddenly felt foolish.

In front of Joe, and most of the others, I didn't mind appearing foolish by playing drunk, but with Chris in the picture, I wasn't sure I wanted to continue this charade. I suddenly felt a burning desire to get sober quick.

"Let me take her home." This time it was Chris. I was getting the same dial tone, from different ends of the spectrum. The words had come from Chris, but they were indistinguishable from Joe's.

"Wait a minute! Nobody tells me what to do. How come everyone is so concerned with...?" I lost my train of thought because Joe had stepped around me and I realized that neither man was listening to me as they were engaged in their own heated conversation.

"I have the situation under control, Chris, so just butt out!" Joe was talking with his size.

"Oh, and I suppose you also want to take her home," Chris said sarcastically.

"All she needs is a good night's rest, to sleep it off."

"She's not going to get much sleep, Joe, with you laying on top of her."

"She's drunk!" exclaimed Joe.

"Yeah. Easy pickings. Every guy here would kill to take her. How come you're the chosen one?"

"You are sick. I'm just going to take her home. She's drunk!"

"Ha! As if that's stopped you before. I always heard that it was a prerequisite with you," accused Chris.

"You goddamn fool! Liz is different!"

"Oh, a step up from your usual bimbo?"

Things were desperate now, Joe was in his face. "You spineless slimeball, just because you can't get a woman to go to bed with you! I should break you in half."

Chris wasn't backing up. So I pushed him back. It felt good.

Both men were looking at me.

I looked at Chris. I looked at Joe. I hated them both. Was it all men I hated?

Chris—God, you don't know what a few words can do. I am sober, and I heard them all. You went from a dream to a dread.

Joe. Noble? I never would have guessed it, but in his own way, he did have integrity. Still, not my idea of a dream, but at least not a nightmare.

What was happening here? How did this come down to a choice? I had totally lost control of the situation I created.

Even as I was thinking, again I was losing their attention as I noticed them eyeing one another. This was my play! I control the script. "Chris, Joe has promised to take me home." It was time for me to get back in the director's chair. "Now go sit down, Chris, you're much more becoming when you're quiet."

Before either man could say a word I turned and headed out the door.

* * *

"How do you work this thing?" I clumsily fumbled with the seat belt, acting like I had never seen such a complicated device in my life.

He was trying to be a good coach from a distance. "Pull it all the way. Yes...no, now put it in the slot."

"Are you talking about the seat belt?"

Oh, he is so cute when he blushes. I had to try to keep him at his color. "I notice you found the slot right away. I had heard you were good." I reached over to grab his seat belt, making sure I grabbed just a little of him also. "And look how tight it is!"

I pointed my toes and leaned back in the seat asking, "Would you do mine for me?"

He buckled my seat belt quickly, but I did notice that he lingered over me for just a second afterward.

Taking a deep breath he asked, "Where do you live?"

"In a house. Oh, it's a nice house that I've lived in for almost four years now, no make that five, maybe four and a half, but it's yellow with white trim." I took a breath. "Why, where do you live?"

"Ah, I'm taking you home, remember? I need an address."

"Don't you have an address?"

"Yes, I have one, but I'm taking you home, and I need yours!"

"Why should I tell you mine, when you won't tell me yours?" I smiled my most diabolical smile.

"Because I'm taking you home, and it's a little hard if I don't know where you live."

"You can tell me. Don't be shy," I coaxed.

He was shaking his head in exasperation.

"I'll take my seat belt off and make you find my slot again," I threatened. "How many times can you find the slot in one night, Joe?"

"You're insufferable! You're giving me a headache."

"Wow! I would have never taken you for an equal opportunity excuse giver."

He had to laugh. Poor Joe, he was more drunk than I was, but I wasn't about to let him know that.

Suddenly there was a change in his face, and for a moment I thought he was going to take my hand. Instead he said, "I've never been so out of control with a woman before. I don't know if I'm coming or going."

"Well, are you going to tell me your address so you can take me home?" I tried my best to make it sound perfectly logical.

He threw up his arms. "You win. I live at 4533 Smith."

"Is that in Rocky River?"

"Yes, it is! Now you have to tell me where you live."

"I live in Rocky River too!"

"Really, where?"

"Get going, and I'll show you."

We were finally moving.

I told him where to turn, and purposely once had him go in a complete circle around a block. He mumbled something to himself but he was doing his best to be patient with me.

"What are you doing? You don't live on my street!" He was finally realizing that this just might be another game.

"Shh!" I quieted him. "Go slow, it's right around here, and my house is hard to find in the dark."

"You've only been living there for five years." I smiled at him as he said this, and immediately he accelerated and after passing about ten houses he quickly pulled into a driveway. I was glad that my seat belt was fastened.

"I'm home!" he said.

"Oh, you coy devil, you were leading me here all along!" I tried to sound sincere, but a giggle or two leaked out.

"I'm tired of games." He rubbed his forehead.

I took his hand down from his forehead and said, "I was hoping the games were about to begin."

"Is this really what you want? Or is it just a game? Or are you just drunk?" he rattled off questions as if he were reading from a list.

"Which answer do you want to hear?"

"Just please tell me where you live so I can take you home."

"I want to spend the night here."

When I got no response, I pushed a little further, "If you're feeling down, I can just sleep on your couch. I sleep in the raw, and I don't need any covers—for I'm quite hot right now."

"God, I'm only human. Please stop this!"

"Do you want me?" I asked.

"Cut it out!" he turned away, pulling his hand from mine.

I slowly unbuckled my safety belt and slide over to his side of the car. I could feel his heavy breathing pass through my body as I made contact with him.

I kissed his cheek, and whispered in his ear, "Do you want me?"

I felt his body tense and I braced myself. But instead of pushing me away he took me into his arms. Kissing me with a passion that drove me further from reality, from actress to fantasy girl, it was at that moment that I knew that I was going to spend the night with him.

He scared me. I was finally able to admit that. His strength. His all-consuming passion. His sexual power. This was his arena now, and I could see no other way but to be dominated.

For a time I felt so out of control. So powerless. Somewhere it had switched. From my newly discovered game to his reality. This was his world. This was what he was about.

But somewhere it changed again for me. We were in his bed, sheets and covers flung over our crumbled clothes on the floor. Two naked bodies, and one bare soul left on the bed. He was on top of me. I was right there. The intensity. I felt his every muscle. I breathed in as he exhaled. My tits felt like they were rockets ready to blast off as his lips brushed over them. The moment. I was in the moment, but somewhere it changed.

I was far away in an instant. From no thoughts—to thinking of my first sexual encounter.

* * *

I was of high school age. I was a senior, but when it came to this I felt like a wide-eyed freshman. I was glad I didn't have to graduate as a virgin.

"I want to make love to you." I can still hear the words from long ago, whispered in my ear. It was the first time.

Feeling fear. Almost panic.

It wasn't hard to say "OK." What was difficult, was whispering to him, "I'm still a virgin."

Henry pretended not to be shocked, but the look on his face made me think otherwise.

"So please be gentle." I tried to smile.

We had waited long enough. We both knew that. It was time.

His body, that I had come to know so well, now seemed so strange as he entered me...slowly at first. Pain. I wanted to scream out. But as his momentum grew I almost became accustomed to the pain. I could feel the wetness between my legs, but I tried not to think that most of it was blood.

Henry was almost as nervous as I was. He was awkward, but gentle. Fumbling around, misplaced limbs and body parts, it seemed it would never end.

Still the steady pace increased. On and on it continued in a perpetual rhythm.

It took everything to hold the scream inside.

I braced myself against the onslaught as all rhythm was lost, and Henry's body quivered and shook above me. Still he pushed harder, plunging himself inside me deeper...until I thought I would break apart. My legs wrapped around him as I hung on.

Amidst the pain, suddenly I felt like someone had broken a tiny warm water balloon deep between my legs, and just as suddenly, it was over. I realized, with a sigh, that he had come.

I had been completely aware of each moment. I had been there from start to finish—an accomplishment I have since found hard to repeat.

* * *

But this memory came back to me just as a thought—which gave way to other, unrelated thoughts, and before I knew it the dam was open. And the wave of thoughts took me far away, to the past, to the future, anywhere but in Joe's bed. A two hundred pound man on top of me, inside me...but I wasn't there.

Numb. Numb to pain, numb to pleasure—it was really all the same.

Joe was doing his best to get me to feel the pleasure, but I was too afraid of having to admit to that past pain, and with it, any past pains. Stay numb to it all, it's easier that way. I felt as if I had a tiny tape loop that ran continuously in my head saying simply, "Stay numb."

I knew the climax was coming, a part of me wanted to be there. I flashed in and out. Most of the time I felt like a spectator. Was this one of those cheep porno flicks? I could only tell myself that yes, it was.

None of it was real.

Thoughts were my only reality.

My thoughts were becoming almost as uncontrollable as my life, and what good was that?

When reality and fantasy merge to become one, is that what we call insanity?

Joe finally rolled off me. I could only think, "Thank God that it's over."

Away. Away. I tried not to convey to Joe that I was running away. But I ran.

I told Joe that the sex was good. I'm sure he was good. I'm sure that if I could have been there one hundred percent we would have both been carried away by the passion and fallen for each other, and went on to live happily ever after.

If only. Only if. The story of my life. It was close, and if things would have been just a little different, it may have worked. Waiting, forever waiting for that one little thing that goes wrong to blame everything on. Something can always be found, however minute. I am an expert at trivialities.

It is said that closeness only counts in hand grenades and sex. I think I am afraid of both.

Perhaps my real fear is that I will give one hundred percent to a relationship and still not be loved.

I turned to see a baffled look on Joe's face as I headed out the door.

* * *

Back in my own bed, more alone than ever, I buried my face in my pillow, waiting for sleep or suffocation, whichever came more quickly.

My alarm clock woke me at six thirty. I didn't need to get up that early, and more importantly, I didn't want to get up that early, but I had forgotten to shut it off. Although it was a Saturday, it was waking me as if it were a workday.

Struggling to get back to sleep was more work than work would have been. After about a half hour I got up.

After I got cleaned up and made myself breakfast, I sat on the couch to watch TV. I think I lasted about three minutes before I fell asleep.

I dreamed about all the things I had planned to do, all the things I had put off until Saturday, all my saved weekly duties that seemed accessible, until last night. It wasn't that I was hung over from the bar—more like hung up.

Even when I awoke from my nap, I still lacked the ambition to do anything. I didn't want to think of what work would be like Monday, having to face Joe—having to face everyone in my office. Faking drunkenness, now I wish I had been drunk so I wouldn't remember the stupid things I did and said.

What would Joe say? Would he be hurt? Of course not, one night stands were common with Joe—I was just another in a long line. But he said I was different. I heard Joe tell Chris that I was different...but I don't want to be. Why does everything I do have to be so special? I can't have casual friends, casual relationships? Why do I always feel the heat of a spotlight on my brow?

I chose Joe over Chris. What would Chris think? I chose Joe over every guy that was in the bar, how did that make them feel? Probably just like they already did—most girls pick Joe over any of them, and they see it happen all the time. So do they think that I'm just like all the other girls? And isn't that what I want? To be average. Normal.

But then do I lose myself?

A new meaning to "lost in thought." Confused in feeling.

Why should I take responsibility for making others feel less than Joe? By choosing one, why do I feel like I'm putting down all others?

A million whys. A billion sighs. As everyone looks for the one answer.

Breaking. Crumbling. Bit by bit. I needed something to hold. I needed someone to hold me together. I needed someone to touch me. To really get through. The one person who could break through, Stephen, and I was terrified to call him. What if he didn't care?

I picked up the phone and dialed the first four digits of his phone number and hung up.

Scolding myself, I dialed again. I listened to the ringing of the phone in a trance. There was a click and his voice was speaking to me. But it wasn't him, it was his answering machine. I started to hang up, but instead I took a deep breath and said, "Hi, this is Liz. Sorry about the late night call. I realized that you couldn't call me the next day because I don't think I ever gave you my number. So anyway, it's 284-6741. Give me a call. Thanks."

I hope he was tired enough last time I talked to him not to see through the white lie—for I was the one who was supposed to call him.

Immediately I went to the basement to do some laundry. I threw in a load, came upstairs and made the bed and straightened my bedroom. I took the clothes from the washing machine and threw them in the dryer, and popped another load in the washing machine. I just entered the living room with a dust rag in hand when the phone rang.

I counted three rings, then picked it up.

"Hello."

"Hi Liz, this is Stephen."

"Stephen who? No, I'm just kidding. How are you?"

"I'm wide awake."

"Oh!" A laugh. "Well I just woke up."

"Suddenly I'm getting very tired."

"Probably tired of me and my crying..."

"You sound great today."

I was feeling much better. "Well, I'm not always crying—just like you're probably not always tired."

"No...not when I'm sleeping—for I dream of being wide awake."

"What do you dream of doing while you're wide awake?"

"Huh?" He laughed.

"You know what I mean!"

"The only way for you to know what my dreams are, is for you to come into one of them."

"Is that an invitation?" I said, trying to sound...uh, sexy.

"I think you would add a definite improvement to my dreams."

"Maybe we could make a dream come true."

"How about tonight? I could work my schedule free for a dream."

He was so easy to be with. To be me. To be emotional. I wasn't "checking" the things I said. It was a free feeling. I felt I didn't have to hold back with him. If I had taken the time to stop and think about it, I would have been terrified. Instead I laughed and said, "My schedule is full of nightmares I wouldn't mind canceling."

I gave him my address.

"Eight o'clock then?"

"Eight sounds great!"

"For a dream."

"For a dream."

I hung up the phone thinking that at least I had gotten a good head start on cleaning my house. Calling him had taken me out of my funk, even if it was only to talk to his machine. But then, talking to the real Stephen, making a date—for tonight! I couldn't wait to see him. To be near him.

Please, don't let me cry tonight. I want a lover— not a counselor. I don't want him to think I'm broken. He does not have to fix me, it's just that he brings out the real me. I no longer have to pretend to have no emotions. He has seen me at my worst, and he actually asked me out! He accepts me for me.

!!!!!!!...When this panic attack ends I will treat this date just like any other...

PART D

GROWING

It's sad to grow up before your time. A child's life is fleeting as it is. With each step, each day's passing, the adult within creeps a little forward. From the child's perspective childhood fades so slowly, almost unnoticeably. A child's life is spent in wonder, yet much of that wonder is directed towards the adults around them. And there is a yearning. A desire to grow up, to leave childhood behind; to leave the awkwardness, the stupidity, the naivete, the smallness. Though it seems every child's wish is to grow up, it's nonetheless a tragedy when one innocent child grows up before his time. To grow in experience, before growing in years. Pains, tragedy, horror are some of the things that can bring about a premature launch into adulthood.

Sometimes an event lasting only a moment can change a life forever. Like nightmares that haunt us upon awakening, there are certain events that we never fully wake from. Dreams that make no sense are easily forgotten upon morning light, but when an event that we classify as reality makes no sense to us, we have trouble forgetting it. It can haunt us for the rest of our life, even if we do our best to bury it in our subconscience. An event that holds us prisoners within ourselves, hardening us on the outside, yet often from that moment on, we never really grow inside. We are aware of the mush on the inside; thus we determine that we must make our exterior tough to protect what's vulnerable underneath.

To a child in the park he is the world. He does not analyze the future, thinking of his coming acne, and what affect it will have on him as a teenager. Tomorrow is something he cannot envision, and

36

thus doesn't care about. He only innocently lives for today. He sees the sun and the swings and he is happy.

The world is all in front of him, and he cannot even imagine the dark. Evil is a game, or a movie, it doesn't really exist to him.

He never notices the figure in the shadows as he runs for the swings. Even when the man steps into view, the small boy only smiles at him, seeing him just as an adult, something he wishes to be himself someday.

The adult speaks. His voice is in hushed whispers and the wind seems to carry it away and play tricks with it. The boy doesn't understand all the words, but laughs—seeing the adult as comical. The adult shows the boy a trick, a quarter disappears, and then he wants to know if the boy has it. Slowly and smoothly the adult places a hand on the little boy's shoulder. The boy feels the weight of the adult's hand, and is suddenly frozen. He does not think about what his mommy told him about strangers, for this adult is not strange, really. He is an adult.

The other hand comes forward. "Where is that quarter?" thinks the boy.

"What's your boy's name?" A voice from behind the boy startles him, and obviously, the adult, for the grip on the boy's shoulder tightens. It was hurting him, but before the boy could say so, he released it and the adult said, "It's not my boy. He just dropped his quarter, and I've been trying to help him find it." That quarter wasn't lost after all, and he holds it out in his hand for the boy to take. "Here," the adult says, "now your mommy won't punish you for losing your quarter."

The little boy grabs the quarter from the big hand without thanks or understanding. He only knows that now he is rich. He runs back to the swings to play, and by the time he thinks to look back, the adult is gone. He thought to thank him for the quarter, but it is too late.

He looks, for the first time, to the other person there. Another adult. He doesn't thank him; does he have any reason to?

"Come on. I'll walk you home." Obediently the boy gets up, and the man walks him home. He was a nice man, but not quite as friendly as the first.

When the boy was safely at his home, and both men were mere memories, never to been seen or heard from again, the boy would think of this day only as a day he was given a quarter. It made him smile even as he grew into an adult. It was a slow trip, but a mostly pleasant one.

An event, but not a tragedy.

CLUTCH

I should have noticed the jeans he was wearing when I let Steve in—at least that he was wearing jeans—but I can't say I did. Maybe if I would have, the request he was going to make wouldn't have taken me by surprise.

After exchanging pleasantries and a quick drink he blurted it right out. "Can you change?"

"I..." I didn't know what to say. Was this a test? I didn't even really know this man, and already he was asking me to change. What was it that he didn't like about me? I wouldn't change to please anyone but me. I knew this crying thing was going to get in our way...

"Into something more comfortable, I mean."

"What?"

"You look gorgeous, but I don't think a dress will do for where I'm taking you."

"You know how long it took me to get ready? What are you telling me? That you're taking me to a mud wrestling match where I'm the main attraction?"

"Something like that." A mischievous smile crept over his face, but it was so inviting.

My dress was off, but my guard was up. "We'll see if you can get me out of these jeans as easily as you got me out of the dress."

"Oh, you're so easy." He laughed.

I couldn't help but notice how much more forced my laugh was than his was.

"Where are we going?"

"Don't you like surprises?"

"Only when they're predictable."

"OK. OK. I get the hint. Have you ever heard of Whirly Ball?
"It better not be some sort of sexual aid!"
"Hah! Sort of a bumper car sport actually."

Bumper car basketball is the way I came to think of it. It turns out that he, and about ten of his friends, had rented the place for a few hours. It was a strange way to meet the friends of the guy you're dating. Literally running into them. It was a strange first date. Not exactly dinner and a movie.

The cars were so hard to control. The game itself took a back seat to the task of ramming into other unsuspecting cars and avoiding surprise bumps. It was so hysterical trying to figure out the strange steering at a moment's notice to try to avoid someone. More often than not I seemed to go in the wrong direction. I laughed almost continuously. I have never before so enjoyed being out of control.

It was a real nice way of getting me to loosen up. It was a first date that was so much more comfortable than first dates usually were. But then it was a first date with Stephen, and I had known it would be like no other.

Stephen was funny, yet he was one of those more serious about actually playing the game. There were a few on each side intent on winning the game, while the rest of us just buzzed around—getting in the way. It was a nice mix of skill and mayhem. With either everyone serious or everyone madcapped, it wouldn't have worked. The evening had a pleasant edge to it.

And we won!

I didn't even realize it had happened. It was suddenly over, and Stephen was hugging me. I guess I didn't keep track of the score, or the time, or whatever you're supposed to keep track of. I didn't even make a score...unless Stephen was my goal. Only time, and maybe a few prayers, would tell.

What is most puzzling, is that I had so much fun in a group type outing. I usually avoid crowds—especially when most of the people are strangers. For much of my life even two has been considered a crowd.

"Alone." Is it possible to have something like that ingrained in one's genes? It's odd that most of my childhood memories are from times when I was alone. It seems strange to me that I used to isolate so much as a kid, but it's a trait I carried with me to adulthood.

I was fairly popular in my school days, but it wasn't something which I strived for. Actually, it's more accurate to say that I ran from my popularity. I never could run fast enough...

We went for a bite to eat, while his friends went to the bar in the same restaurant. We laughed often over dinner and talk flowed freely.

I told him of my eight children in different parts of the country, and one in the oven; and he told me he was studying us, as member of an alien race who were responsible for starting world war one, two, and three. Then he looked at his watch and said, "Oops! Not yet for number three."

I said we laughed a lot!

I knew I wanted to go home with him, but every time I thought about the possibility I grew panicky. He rescued me from my fears by suggesting we join his friends in the lounge.

With loud music playing, and everyone seemingly talking at once, about people and situations I knew nothing about, I soon lost track of the conversation. For the first time, around Stephen and his friends, I felt like a stranger.

I wanted to get out. But Stephen was having such a good time. I had to admit that most of my problem with the situation was that I wanted him all for myself. But these were his friends, and what kind of first date was that?

I soon became lost in my head. I no longer even pretended to be listening to anyone.

Why would a man ask a woman out to a first date such as this? Where was the romance? Perhaps he wanted none, at least where I was concerned.

But as I thought it over, I gradually came to my senses. This night out with "the gang" must have been planned in advance. They had to rent the court to play Whirly Ball on. It was a spur of the moment thing, his asking me out. Maybe he just really wanted to see me, and since he already had plans, he thought it would be wise to bring me along. I have to admit I haven't exactly been the easiest person to stay in touch with. He probably would have contacted me long before this if I had only given him my phone number.

Still, he could have asked...although it would have been more romantic for him to search for me. To call every conceivable combination of phone numbers until I answered the phone. To knock on every door, in a fifty block radius from the bar we met, until I opened the door and invited him in to live happily ever after with me.

Oh, he was so great. He was so natural, he did things for the fun of it, not caring how he looked. If he said something foolish he didn't hide from it. If he said something profound he didn't flaunt it. God, I had to have him.

But did he want me? If he didn't, I knew I had the skills to make him want me. It worked on Joe. But Joe had already wanted me. The foolish fake drunkenness thing I did was only to allow myself the freedom to say yes. And actually, it had almost chased him away— to the point where I practically had to beg him to do something he had been trying to talk me into for years.

I knew I was very good looking, but I guess being sexy was something different—something I couldn't quite grasp. If Stephen was looking for sexy, I wasn't sure I could deliver. But I wanted him, and I would have to try. But would trying to be something that I really didn't know how to be just chase him away? Stephen was so powerful he would see through any games. I didn't just want to be friends, and God knows I didn't want sex. I just wanted something long lasting, without the fear of expectations or the threat of abandonment.

Romance—a strange concept. I guess I was looking for it, but unsure of exactly what it was. I knew it took two, thus maybe I wasn't living up to my end of it. It never occurred to me that it also might be an elusive concept for Stephen as well.

Perhaps it was up to me.

He had already given me so much. If I could just reach out of myself to lead this relationship into a romance that possibly either of us had only dreamed of, I could return the favor. And I wouldn't mind benefitting from my lead.

If I could only...*get out of my head*!

In a flash I pictured myself sitting alone in the bar.

Gone and forgotten? At least they were still here. At least he was still here, them I didn't care about.

Walking over to Stephen, I put my arm around him.

Looking at me, he said, "Hi there. Sorry, are you getting tired?"

"A little, I guess. Why, do I look tired?"

"A little, I guess." He smiled and my heart and stomach momentarily changed places. He didn't need candlelight and obscure poetry to be romantic. His smile was enough.

I had to smile back.

"You ready to go?" He rubbed my neck.

"Oh, that feels good." But I knew he didn't believe me because I tensed up when he did it. It wasn't that I minded it, it was more that it took me by surprise.

We said good-bye to his friends, and I realized that I remembered very few of their names. They were just faces in a crowd to me; names in the phone book; background noise.

I wished for a gorgeous full moon to greet us as we stepped outside. But there was no moon, and a thick layer of cloud cover from horizon to horizon obscured even the twinkling stars.

As we walked toward his car I matched his step and gently nuzzled my shoulder into his side. Taking a deep breath and letting out a small sigh I said, "The clouds like a blanket, that covers us from the twinkling eyes of the nightly stars, leaving us all alone, just the two of us, on this desolate place we call 'earth.'"

He looked up to the sky, but said nothing.

In his car I thought about the seat belt stunt I played on Chris. I had to laugh.

"What's so funny?" he asked.

Without thinking, I said, "Differences."

"Differences in what?"

"Everything. Nothing is the same. Nothing stays the same. Each snowflake is different from every other. Each snowflake changes; it melts, it crystallizes, it becomes part of a snowball. All is ever changing. Yet, all is one. Everything is connected. The whole picture never changes, though the individual brush strokes are moving constantly."

"Different guy, same scenario?"

He did it again. I don't know why his seeing through me constantly surprised me. That was what I meant, wasn't it? Maybe I just liked his answers better than mine.

"Actually I was referring to my wall..."

"Your wall?"

"Yes." I slowly nodded. "My wall of ice. It is thick, encasing my being, like an igloo. Along comes someone. Finally, someone warm enough to melt this barrier. Only...once my ice has melted, the ice is now water, and the igloo only changes into a moat around me. And I find the one who has melted my igloo can't swim, nor can he fly. So my wall is still just as effective, keeping me separate and distant."

"Maybe in the spirit of friendship each of us can stretch our arms across that moat and join hands. Can you meet me halfway?"

"Friendship. But for anything else we have to reach further, to connect more than our hands. We need to breathe the same air, our hearts to find the same rhythm."

"That's assuming we want more than friendship..."

I pulled myself closer. We were at a red light, so I touched his cheek and gently turned his head toward me. Lifting myself slightly up and out of the seat I kissed him.

There was no response. He didn't pull away, and he didn't kiss me back.

I felt a bit foolish, but I was determined. I stayed near him, looking intently into his eyes. I let my fingertips run under his chin.

"I'm crazy about you," I blurted out.

He looked at me. But his eyes were blank. He was not smiling. God, how I needed to see his smile at this point.

After a while he simply said, "I'm sorry."

I grew dizzy.

"The light has changed, it's a green light...I have to go!"

I couldn't move.

"Please!" he said as he gently pushed me back into my seat and drove on.

I felt embarrassed, helpless, and so confused. Stephen, Stephen, you have got to want me. You don't know what it means to me...

I couldn't say anything. I wanted to ask him what was wrong. Was it something I said, something I did? Was he not attracted to me? Was he seeing someone else? Did he rule out any romantic possibilities with me the moment he saw me crying?

What did I do?

What didn't I do?

I was part of the ever-changing universe, I could be what he wanted!

My mind would not turn off, my mouth would not turn on. He drove me home in silence.

It was in my driveway that I finally summoned the courage to speak. "Come in for a cup of coffee?"

"No. I really can't."

"Come on. It's still early."

"I think you want more than I do."

"Just coffee." I laughed away the tears. "I just want you to come in for a cup of coffee."

"You want a lot more than that!"

"I just...I don't want to be alone tonight."

"And I just want to be friends."

"Not for sex. It's just been a bad week. I need a friend."

"A friend, or a lover?" His eyes looked far into mine.

"I...I don't know." Why couldn't I lie and tell him what he wanted to hear? What did he want to hear? If only I knew!

He said nothing, and I, no longer able to bare the silence, said, "I guess I had hoped that we could be both."

"I am sorry. I don't feel an attraction to you."

"What can I do?" I pleaded to him.

"Just be yourself, and accept things the way they are."

"That's bullshit!"

"I'm sorry you feel that way."

"Quit apologizing! I don't need your sympathy."

"I...don't...know what to say."

"Just say you'll try!"

"I don't want to lead you on."

"I need you."

"And I'm willing to be there for you. As a friend."

"Fuck you!"

"I'm sorry..."

As I got out of his car I slammed the door so hard I nearly fell over.

The tears started coming as I climbed up my stairs. I was thankful that I had saved my tears for after Stephen had gone.

I could not take it. No more.

What was I to do? How could I go on?

My life was a lie. I was stuck. Nothing would ever change. No matter how hard I tried, it never worked out.

I knew I needed to go to bed. Maybe my dreams could take me away, out of my life. Far away from reality is where I needed to be. To run. No looking back. To run free, escape.

But there was nowhere to go. Nowhere that I hadn't already tried. One can only run so far. Running from dead end to dead end, one's legs eventually grew tired, the will faded, the heart died.

I knew I needed to try to sleep. Sleep was far from my mind, so I went up to the attic. Cobwebs, dusty, old, long unopened boxes—I felt at home.

I found an old photo album. My family. I was very little in all the pictures. I was younger, they were proof of happier times. I wasn't always this screwed up.

I flipped through page after page, searching. My hands had already begun to tremble when I finally found what I was looking for. It had taken a while. God, it had taken too long!

A picture. It was just a picture like all the rest. In this particular picture I was sitting on a lawn. I really couldn't tell where the picture was taken, it looked like it could have been anywhere.

This picture was a bit different from most of the rest. It was what I was looking for—a sign of a happier time. In this picture I had a smile on my face. But it troubled me more than anything. Why had it taken so long to find a simple smile on my face? My childhood had been a happy one. Why wasn't I smiling in most of these pictures?

I turned the pages more slowly now. I could remember the pictures from seeing them before, but I don't remember the times they were taken. They all seemed so different now. I felt disconnected. This little girl in the picture with the grim face was not me. This was not my childhood. None of it seemed real.

I stopped on one picture for a moment. I felt a tear trickle down my cheek. It was a normal picture. But I found that I could not get myself to turn the page. I looked at the picture more closely. I was sitting in my father's lap. My mother must have taken this picture, since she wasn't in it. My father had a forced smile on his face, and my smile must have been swallowed. I had a vision of my mother there, taking the picture. Me, in my dad's lap. My mother watching, knowing. Me and my dad, alone in the picture. Alone. A shiver crept up and washed over my spine. I felt myself swallowing repeatedly until my throat went dry. I took a deep breath and closed my eyes.

Feeling myself growing calm, I opened my eyes. The picture was still there. But it was changing—right before my eyes. It was moving. We were moving, my father and me. We swirled around and around as my eyes blurred slowly out of focus. Before I knew what was happening I felt a part of the picture—not part of my past, but I was now in the picture. My dad was still moving. He rose above me. My head was spinning, but now he was still. I could feel him there, so close. I screamed loud and long, but the image of him would not fade and go away. I saw the little girl screaming, no, I am the little girl. A rage builds inside. I scream. God, I scream until my throat is raw, but it does no good.

I am suddenly back in my attic. I try to clear my head, but I hear a voice in my head. I cannot block it out. It is his voice, I quiver as it echoes in my head, "You loved it."

NO! But as my hand moves, to push this nightmare memory away, it comes to rest where I feel the dampness. I become sickeningly aware of the moistness between my legs. I am wet.

No. It can't be. What is wrong with me?

I can still see the hate in my mother's eyes, not for my father...but for me. It was my fault—why did I let it happen?

Staggering to my feet, I use a stack of boxes to support myself and they go tumbling over, sending dust flying everywhere. I feel so dirty, but I don't even notice the dust.

In a desperate need of air I shove open a window. As I breathe in desperate gasps I see the dust in front of my eyes, and can almost feel it speckling my lungs.

I climb out the window and onto the roof, to escape the dust. But I cannot escape my skin. I can never escape from the real filth.

I hold my head, trying to hold it together, trying to push back in the thoughts, the newly discovered memories that had lay dormant for so long, like those dusty boxes in the attic, long forgotten, yet always there, waiting...

I look over the rooftops and say in a hushed voice, "Nowhere left to run."

Then the answer comes.

My head clears.

One final step.

I look up to the sky, to see a small break in the clouds. A few stars shine between the clouds. The clouds are moving, soon the gap will be closed.

From one moment to the next, life is just a decision.

I look to the sidewalk below. It doesn't look too far down, only a lifetime or so. If the pavement were water, it would be said to be as smooth as glass. Like an ocean, calm, before the storm.

Meanwhile an inner storm raged. I longed for that smooth inner peace. Calm after the storm. Calm during the storm. It was only a choice. All life was a matter of making choices. This one was simple, inevitable. Turn the page. Or put down the book.

One final step. Into a dive over the edge. Head first. It will be quicker.

As I feel the blood rush to my head, the wind racing through my hair, I am reminded of my impending freedom.

I don't scream, but about halfway down I close my eyes.

THE END

PART E

JUST SUNDAY

I go to church every Sunday. It's a small congregation. I know them all. Some are friends.

On this particular Sunday I had on a new dress, one that exceeded the limits of my budget, and although not one to show off, I did think I looked nice in it.

But it was after church, while pumping gas, in my new dress, that I got touched in an almost mystical way.

My thoughts were a million miles away as my tank filled. I was standing too close and three big, obvious drops of gas splashed out onto the front of my dress.

I said nothing, trying to remain impervious to the minor catastrophe, but for some persistent tears that crept out from the corner of my eyes.

As I turned to leave, the man pumping gas next to me, whom I had not even noticed before said, though his eyes seemed sad and his smile might have been forced, "Peace be with you."

Words can be heard hundreds of times in certain contexts, but when placed outside of their familiar surroundings they can take on a whole new depth of meaning.

I got into my vehicle without acknowledgment, for all he knew his words went unheard, but maybe for the smile that possibly flashed across my face. I drove down the road, no longer lost in thought; no longer aware of the gas smell permeating my dress, yet the tears still came. They flowed freely. I cried only for the peace within me, finally found.

At times that it seems no one cares, perhaps these feeling are correct, for maybe these are times we find ourselves caring about what is unimportant.

CHAPTER II

FELT

The feeling of fear that I awoke with was not unusual for me, but it slowly drifted away, and numbness crept in as I read the morning paper.

I knew that girl. A picture on the front page of the newspaper. Small article. It said she was dead. Suicide.

At first I denied it was her. Then I realized that the picture was that of a slightly younger, happier, less uptight girl than the one I had seen two nights ago. But it was the same girl. She had been intense, so much so it had scared me. So intense...it led to suicide.

I set the paper down. She had killed herself on the night of our date. It couldn't have been long after I had dropped her off.

* * *

"How's it going, Steve?"

"Fine."

"Hey, Stevie!"

"What's up Joe."

"Hello, Stephen."

"Hi, Mr. Rendch."

"How are you Steve...anything exciting happen recently Steve-boy?...what's shaken?...how've you been, Stevie?"

Throughout the day my words slipped between clenched teeth, and I answered them all. Nothing's wrong. I'm okay I said for my benefit as much as theirs. By the end of the day I realized that no one could tell a thing was wrong with me. By the end of the week, neither could I.

* * *

A knock upon my door. The opening of which reveals two police officers.

Suddenly I'm down at the police station, still in my underwear, with about five policemen confronting me with accusations of pushing Liz out of her bedroom window.

The last question that still rings in my brain even after awakening from the nightmare was from one huge cop who was in my face screaming, "What was the sex like!?"

I lay awake in bed wondering if Liz left a suicide note. I imagine what it might say.

Was I the last person she had contact with? Was I the reason? I knew there had to be more to her decision, but maybe I was the last straw. Maybe if I would have been more understanding. Maybe if I would have given in. Maybe....just maybe...Liz might be alive today.

* * *

"On and on this life goes,
I hide these things I need to know.
Deep inside they tend to grow...
Until off my head will blow.

Denying one's feelings from the self,
Piling them up like dusty old books
Until the lack of room on the shelf
Sends them tumbling down, we're forced to look."

"Are you trying to tell me something?" She handed the paper across her desk to me.

"Huh?"

"In the margin, see the little poem scribbled there?"

I read the little scribbles. I had never seen them before. It was my handwriting.

"Is that an official part of the report?" She gave me a profane smile.

"It was...my nephew...she, ah—he must have gotten a hold of this before I handed it in, I..."

"I think Quadex would be a little antsy if they thought we were covering something up. If this had gotten through to them it may have blown the whole deal."

"Keep your papers away from the kids, and please check them over before you hand them in to me. There is no excuse for this!" Her anger peaked, then she dismissed me with a turn of her back saying, "No need to retype this page, I already had Sharon take care of it—just get rid of it so no one else sees it."

My hands were shaking as I left her office. I don't think she noticed.

When had I written that? I often scribble in the margins of the rough drafts, but the finished version? I crumpled up the page and stuffed it in my pocket, not daring to look at it again.

I had to get a hold on myself. I knew the poem wasn't about any Quadex deal, it was about the girl. But I didn't even know her, and she didn't know me. How could I even begin to feel guilty about her death, surely it had nothing to do with me! It was all coincidence. Life was full of one bloody coincidence after another.

What was it about that girl? When I dropped her off that night did some part of me know her potential for suicide? Did I see the same tendency in myself, and is that why I couldn't be around her? Did I really relate to her on such a deep level? I know that in some way or another I always feel that I can relate to a person. Any person. To everyone else, some person can seem totally opposite of me in every respect, but leave it to me to find, and feel, that one thread of similarity that runs between us. Was the similarity I felt with the girl a tendency towards suicide? Was that why I let myself be chased away by her. She was a beautiful girl, smart, easy to talk to—so why did I push her away? What was I so afraid of? Was it that we were just getting too close? Too close? I never let anyone get too close. People let me in, but had I ever let anyone in to see the real me? Did I fear that she knew the real me, because she was just like me? But one thing I knew for sure is that she really didn't know herself, so she couldn't know me. No, perhaps the fear was more like she would bring out the me that I'd been denying even to myself. Is that what I brought out in her? Is that why she's dead now? Maybe we could have handled it together. If only I would have given her a chance. If only I had given myself a chance...

I thought of my mother. My mother was nothing like the girl. And I knew, deep down, neither was I.

Yet, wasn't everybody alike?

* * *

I had a dream that I was falling.

Falling. On and on. Forever falling. It seemed that I was destined to fall for eternity. At first I was panicked, but after a while I almost accepted my plight. Not that I was comfortable, but I couldn't embrace my terror forever, could I?

When suddenly I hit!

Splat.

I lay there.

What they say about falling and landing in dreams is a fallacy—for I was still alive. Both in my dream and real life, it seemed I had endured the fall.

A voice not unlike his own was talking, "Don't worry about landing, it's only an instant of pain, then it's all over. It's the fall that will get you! When in a state of trepidation we think at a rate of a thousand thoughts per second."

I knew that I was alive, yet I lay there motionless. I couldn't move. It's almost as if I was paralyzed.

Something inside me screamed, "Move! Get up!" but my will to listen to that voice seemed to be gone.

I lay there, and just as I accepted my falling, I would learn to accept my immobility.

I awoke in a state of shock more than I had at any time in my dream.

CHAPTER III

HELD

A cool hand upon my forehead and a voice that said, "Dave, you ok?"

My insides jumped through the roof, but on the outside all that gave away my surprise was a muttered, "What the..."

"We're due up."

"OK." I climbed to my feet, pretending not to see her hand.

"You were really lost in thought there. Thinking about anything special?"

I honestly couldn't remember what I had been thinking about. "Work," I lied.

I was about to play doubles; with a partner I had never played with before, but knew, vaguely. We were playing against a team, of which I knew the woman quite well, Elise—she was one of Joan's old friends—and a guy I knew not at all. I don't think I had ever even seen this guy around before, and from the way he acted around Joan, I doubt they had met before either. Maybe he was new. Well, if he was, maybe Sally and I could give him a good initiation into the tennis club.

It started off slow; the rallying was a bit unorthodox, as the new guy didn't seem to know what to do. He hit many a ball on to other courts—and this was just the warm-ups.

He seemed amiable enough, he would joke every time a hit went astray, nothing obnoxious, just a funny-worded embarrassed apology.

I must admit to getting a little weary, and possibly he sensed this, for he said, "Rallying's not my strong point. Do you want to just get started?"

I looked at Sally. She nodded and said, "Let's just get this over with."

"Sure, why not?" I yelled over. It was the shortest rallying I had ever done, and although I wasn't sure that I was warm, I knew that Sally and I should have no problem putting them away without much effort. For I knew that Sally was a level above that of Elise, and the new guy—from the way he was rallying—he was probably not as good as Elise.

"We should get this over quick and easy," I remember thinking. Good thing I don't always say what I think, for instead I told Sally, "You can't always judge someone by the way they rally."

We let beginners serve first, it's a little tradition we have at the club, by purposely blowing the volley for serve.

Well, we had a quick wake up call. Without taking any practice serves he served three aces in his first game and won, game—fifteen.

"You don't have to rally much when you serve up aces." Sally tossed me a ball.

"Let's see if he can return service."

He turned out to play a fast, power type game. He took the net with ease and put shot after shot away as we tested him there.

We were down, they had the momentum, and this new guy continued to gain confidence. So Sally and I had a little strategy session in-between sets.

"We have to keep him off the net," Sally said between breaths.

"He's too quick, he's taking the net when he has no right to...let him take the net, now let's test his patience. Lob."

Sally just nodded.

"Elise will never be able to keep up. That will force him back to cover for her."

The plan worked, but only after a real gut check on our part. For Elise stepped up her game and fired back each lob into our corners, and we had to claw and scrape for each and every point. Somewhere the tide had turned and we eeked out enough games to force a tiebreaker for the match.

Sally and I dug in and won the tiebreaker without too much trouble.

"Nice game." I shook the new guy's hand. "I'm Dave. Dave Snow."

"Thanks. I'm Steve Mioyu."

"That was quite a workout," Sally interjected as we all walked off the court together.

"Best I've had in a long time." Steve laughed.

"You gave us a little start there!" I relayed.

"What, did you think I was having a heart attack?"

"Don't worry, Steve, we do have quite a few doctors in the club." I patted him good-naturedly on his back.

"You do realize, Steve, that if you had won we would've had to kick you out of the club!?" Sally joined in.

"Me?" Steve stopped in his tracks. "It was all my partner's doing! Elise was the one responsible for us winning any games."

"Right," sighed Elise. "I didn't even touch the ball that first game, and only after because *they* decide to pick on me all night." Elise pointed an accusing finger at Sally and I.

"Pick on you! Look at that, Dave, she's so paranoid she acts like we plotted and planned against her." Sally threw a wink my way.

"Seriously, Elise, that's the best I've seen you play." I don't think I totally kept the wonder out of my voice.

I don't know where the suggestion came from, but somehow all four of us ended up at Mackeely's across the street from the club. I know that drinks were suggested first, but Steve was hungry, having come straight from work, and we humanely steered him away from the moldy sandwiches served at the tennis bar.

The "new guy" turned out to be a nice guy. He was funny, and a genuine warmth came from him. He was different from most the other guys at the club, he didn't cry and complain about losing, and he didn't seem stuck up, which was unique indeed.

Elise was her usual quiet, sweet self. She had been one of Joan's only friends that I could really get along with.

Then there was Sally, whom I've not quite figured out. She was OK, I guess, but we had both been members in the tennis club for a long time and I had never felt the urge to get to know her better. She had the unnerving habit of acting like she and one of us, seemingly taking turns, was in with her on a private joke. She always seemed to be talking with one particular person, and at the remaining two.

The conversation was lively, and all four of us seemed to have fun. Elise was more talkative than I have ever seen her. Maybe it's not a fair comparison, though, because the only other times I have really talked to her was when Joan was around, and Joan had a way of bringing anybody down.

Once, when I got up to get a round of drinks because the waitress was too slow for our thirst, Steve was saying something about maybe Elise's name being the title of a song, she said, no, not that she knew, and he said something about a letter and a cure as I was walking away, but I really didn't catch it.

I don't know if it was that Steve's food finally came, or the fact that our conversation had somewhere turned to baseball, that eventually chased off the girls.

After the girls had left I asked him, "Sally's hot, isn't she?"

"Not bad. Not bad at all."

"Man, what a body. She's single, too."

"How about Elise?" Steve asked. "Is she single, too?"

"Yeah, she is," I said. "You don't know her?"

"Not really." Steve shrugged. "To tell you the truth, the only one of the three of you I knew at all was Sally. And actually she is a friend of a friend."

I winked at him. "So you after that Sally?"

"No, no," he said. "I don't think she's my type."

"Oh." Mentally I took a step back. "But Sally's got the body. Man, what a body. Right?"

"Oh, that's one thing you're definitely right about."

"Hey, she may be a stuck-up bitch, but any man can put up with that for a night, huh?" I smiled.

Steve's plates were cleared, and still we sat talking over coffee, I having long given up on the drinks.

I asked him, "You too sore to play a game of tennis tomorrow?"

"Singles?" he asked.

"Why not?"

"Maybe I can force these legs to move two days in a row." He let out an exaggerated moan.

I promised to call for a court.

* * *

He met me after work again. I quickly beat him four straight sets. He was definitely moving a little slower tonight. Seeing that it was a Friday, he had to run right after we were through. Probably had a date. I didn't ask. I knew that I had nothing but an empty apartment to go home to. But as he waved good-bye, I couldn't help smiling, knowing that I had made a friend.

And with Joan out of my life, the thing I needed most right now was a friend.

Steve turned out to be a good friend, as I saw him quite often. We seemed to know a lot about each other by now, but I had never directly brought up Joan. So I was surprised when he brought her up one night.

"How long have you and Joan been separated?"

I didn't know what to say. How did he find out? Finally, I said, "Who told you?"

"You did...in so many words."

"If you've really kept clear of the rumor mill, you are very perceptive!"

"You only mention her every other sentence."

"No..." I vehemently shook my head.

"And always in the past tense."

"What, you think she's dead?"

"No. Usually someone talks about one who has died in a much different tone than one who has left, even if they use the same words."

"Sometimes I think it would have been easier on me if she would have died," I couldn't help but admit.

"How long has it been?" Steve questioned.

"Let's see..." I thought for a second. "We were married for almost six years."

When I said nothing else, Steve looked a little confused, then smiled as if at a private joke, and said, "How long have you been divorced?"

"Just two months now, but we've been separated for a little over a year."

"I'm sorry."

"Oh, I guess I just didn't want to let go."

"I've heard mothers say that the pain of childbearing can pale in comparison to the heartbreak of their child leaving the home for the first time."

"And that can be on good terms." I sighed.

"Not always, but I'm not sure that helps."

"What do you mean?" I didn't follow his reasoning. There were times, it seemed, Steve talked in riddles.

"Sometimes leaving on the best of terms is even more heart-wrenching."

"I can't believe that!"

"Take a look at you and Joan."

"Do I have to?" I joked.

"No..." his voice trailed off.

"I was joking!" I let out what must have sounded like a halfhearted laugh. "Make your point."

"Just that I take it that Joan left you, and you would still be together if it was up to you."

"Is it that obvious?" I asked.

"Sometimes." Then with a quiet voice he went on, "Who do you think is taking it harder?"

"She...I don't tend to...I mean..." I just couldn't get the words out. Finally, when he didn't say anything, and after a few deep breaths I admitted, "I guess that I have."

It took a while to sink in, but then I stated, "Oh, I get your point, sometimes when you're angry at someone it makes it easier to leave.

So leaving on good terms is sometimes harder than leaving on bad. She was the angry one."

The thoughts of a marriage counselor we had been seeing when we were still "trying to make it work" came back to me. It was the same kind of logic. When we brought up about how we fought before each one of my business trips, she explained to us that many couples unconsciously did this, because it made it more bearable to depart. "There is nothing wrong with it, it's common behavior." I remember her saying.

But I must have mistakenly repeated those words I remembered out loud, for I saw the look in Steve's eyes and realized I must have spoken. "I didn't mean the marriage..." I tried to explain, "I meant leaving angry. The marriage had plenty wrong..."

What had been wrong with the marriage? I loved her. Didn't she still love me? Sure, we weren't always as close as we could be, but who was? Or who wants to be? Everybody needs space.

I gave all that I could give, and it wasn't enough. She needed more, always more than I was willing, or could, give. She always thought I was withholding from her; I knew that I was giving all I could. It just wasn't enough.

I must have been in a funk for a while, for I didn't even notice Sally coming over to our table. "Hi, guys. What brings the two tennis pros to this side of town?"

"We were getting tired of tennis, and we heard that you might be here!" Steve smiled.

"Ah, the rumors about me, only some of which are true. Hey, rumor has it that you two are playing a lot of tennis lately, thinking of turning pro?"

"That's an insult!" Steve looked around as if embarrassed, and said, "I already am a pro! I just don't accept money."

"Oh," laughed Sally. "And Dave?"

"He's the one who tries to pay me to play with him."

After Sally stopped laughing I felt I had to get a quip in. "The only thing I give him is sore muscles from chasing my winners."

"He may be quiet, but when he speaks...people listen." Steve nodded my way.

"And laugh!" giggled Sally.

"Sometimes I'm just a little lost in thought. At least I think I am..." I said in a cartoonish voice.

"He's thinking about our next doubles match," said Steve.

"Oh yea? And just when might that be? I think Elise would be willing," Sally guessed.

"Ah, a rematch!" I chided.

"You name the night!" Steve threw it back to Sally's court.

"Well, seeing as you two fellows caught me off guard and I don't have my little schedule book, why don't you give me a call and we'll set up a time over the phone." She scrawled her number on a napkin and handed it to Steve.

I reached up my hand from underneath the table, then when I realized she was intending to give her number to Steve, I quickly made as if all I wanted was to scratch my head. I looked away, trying to hide my embarrassment.

"Hey, I better warn you, you two aren't going to get off so easily next time." Steve waved a threatening finger, first at me, then at Sally. "That first match was just a warm-up."

"That is a threat! Because he knows that we don't want to have to warm up with him again," said Sally as she gave me a little clap.

I excused myself to go to the bathroom as they continued to talk. Steve mentioned something about tennis elbow as I was walking away, but I didn't catch it. Man, I hope he wasn't trying to act like a doctor. How I had hated my dating days, all the phoniness. Besides, I knew pretending to be a doctor wouldn't impress Sally, she had almost married one once, and he hadn't treated her well—now I think she even hated her family physician.

When I returned, again lost in thought, they seemed to be lost in conversation, so I made up some excuse that I had to be going and said my good-byes, I'm sure they didn't care. I went home alone. To an empty apartment, again.

PART F

BETWEEN EARTH AND HEAVEN

I am in a cloud. Others don't notice, not really.

I guess that it's more noticeable when someone is on a cloud. Now that you can't miss! But me, I'm easily passed by, for I live in a cloud—keeping me covered. I cannot see out very well, and those on the outside have trouble seeing in. It's not like I want someone to break through to me. I prefer to be left alone.

I function. Sometimes I don't know how. Or why.

Each shallow breath only seems to accentuate the heaviness in my chest. For my cloud is inside as well as out.

I know that nothing can dispel my cloud, I shall take it to the grave. I often visualize my grave. Waiting up on a hill. Silent. Peaceful.

I have dreams where I am laying on the grass, tombstone at my head. I can't figure out if I'm already dead in the dream, or if I'm just relaxing there...waiting.

It is probably the most peaceful dream I have had in the last two years. No squealing brakes. No crunching metal. No screams. Only silence. Peaceful, calm, silence.

I always focus on my smile in the dream. A feeling of belonging washes over me as I am lying there between my two sweethearts.

* * *

My cloud does move once in a while. It will blow, unceremoniously away, but never too far. I am always aware of its presence, somewhere nearby, although it may temporarily be hiding. For it always returns.

"Things will get better." I have heard sentiments like that often enough to make me want to scream.

"You are a survivor." I am weak.

It is the weakness in me that makes me a survivor.

I am afraid.

Almost always.

The thing that is silly is that I have nothing to fear, not anymore.

Still, terror grips me. It is the one thing that isn't modified by my cloud. It rips the haze away and allows me to see and, worse yet, others to see me.

Others tell me there will again come a day when I care about life, but they are stupid. I care too much! I am the only one who realizes that, and I will take that shameful knowledge to the grave.

My selfishness is what keeps me from that peaceful grave, where I belong. I belong next to my husband and son, in life—and in death. But it is not a perfect world. Far from it.

I am left alone.

Sometimes the wind blows my cloud a bit to the side, but once the wind actually blew somebody through.

He saw me, and I saw him. The cloud had no effect. I didn't freak out, and more surprisingly, neither did he.

It was simple. I don't even remember what he or I said. With his eyes, and not through his mouth, came expressions from his soul.

I understood, and I knew that he did too. As impossible as it is to explain my feelings of the crash, it was equally impossible to explain what happened between me and this stranger.

Maybe it's as simple as he didn't need or expect an explanation. He didn't say anything, not really...and neither did I. But somehow that was enough. Somehow that was everything.

He didn't know anything about me. Nothing. And he looked at me without caring to see all my baggage. He only saw me, and for the first time, in a very long time, I wasn't scared.

In his accepting eyes I saw God.

As my cloud clings to me, or perhaps it is the other way around, I am finally able to realize that when I do go to take my place on the hill, amongst the only two people I will ever love, I will leave this cloud back on earth, where it belongs.

HELD

In the locker room Steve cornered me. "Hey, Dave, so what's with sticking me with Sally the other night?"

"What do you mean?" He had taken me by surprise.

"You ditched me!"

"Hey, I thought you wanted me to leave!" I explained.

"Oh, come on! I never gave you any type of hint that I wanted to be alone with her!"

"But she gave you her phone number!"

"Oh, yes..." Steve's voice suddenly went soft, and looking around he said, "But did I ask for it?"

They had seemed like they were getting along so well. "I just assumed..."

"Well..." interrupted Steve, "next time ask me if your assumption is correct."

"So you don't like her?" I asked.

"What are you, matchmaker? Yes, I like her. She's a nice person, just a little too pushy for me."

"See there! She must have read the same signs I did." I suppressed a laugh. "You're just blind to love!"

"Yea, she read the signs..." Sighing and taking a breath, Steve said, "She figured it was I who urged you to leave!" Then, Steve couldn't help laughing himself.

With that we went out to our doubles match, where, this time they beat us in a tiebreaker.

"Mackeely's again?" asked Steve afterward.

"Look at him, always hungry!" Smiled Elise.

We spent several hours at Mackeely's in which I spent very little time thinking about Joan. But then I went home. Alone.

"Why did she leave me?" I must ask myself that a hundred times a day, so when Steve asked me that same question you think I would have known what to say.

It was three days later. It was after watching a basketball game, we were sitting, having drinks at the bar. Charlotte had lost to the Cavaliers, 102-82. The question came out of nowhere. Well, I guess I had been the one to point out that Joan's cooking was better than that at any of the many restaurants I have since tried. Still, the question hit me like a blow to the back of the head. "Why did she leave?" was all he said.

"Yesterday," was all I could manage.

"Yesterday, or a thousand yesterdays. The difference is only a frail memory's trace of forgotten history," spoke Steve.

"No." I shook my head, not really hearing, or following him. "The song 'Yesterday' by the Beatles. The first few days after she left I played it over and over on the stereo. It was almost romantic. I don't really think I believed she had gone for good. She just left."

I gathered myself and answered Steve's original question. "I'm not really sure why she left. She gave me many reasons. I'm not sure if I believed any one of them. I know that I didn't understand them." A chord of irony rung in my mind. "Huh, that's funny!"

"What's that?" Steve's voice was a gentle whisper now.

"Well, I say I don't understand her reasons for leaving, but that is the one from her that I heard the most—that she didn't understand me."

He only nodded, I'm not sure he really understood. How could he!? I said, "Do you know how much that hurts?"

"No," he admitted.

I looked up at him, a little surprised at his response, his honesty. I saw his eyes; I saw the pain in them. I think I saw a tear forming in the corner of his eye, and quickly I looked away, making sure not to look back there the rest of the night.

"It hurt so bad. I don't think she knows how much that hurt me. I've known her for nine years...and she says she doesn't know me."

"Wow. What did you say to that?"

"I just told her that she never tried."

"Oh." His voice sounded sad, and very far away.

"She said that that was how she felt about our whole marriage—that I never tried. That I never really cared."

I watched a tiny bubble rise to the top on my glass, where it hung on for perhaps fifteen seconds before popping. "She left after saying that. I was hurt. I couldn't say anything. I just watched her walk out the door without saying a word. That night...was the first time I cried since I can remember. Afterward I called her up at her mother's. I told her that I didn't even know myself. I told her I wanted her to know the real me, but that I wasn't sure who that was."

Shifting back to the present I said, "It was a damn nightmare."

I could hear Steve swallow before saying, "Do you?"

I just gazed into the wall, not understanding.

"Care?" he finally said.

"Funny." I didn't laugh. "But I told her that. It was one of the last things I said to her that night. I told her that she may be right about not knowing me, but she was wrong in saying that I don't care. I told her that was all I did care about—'us.' After I told her, the line was quiet for the longest time, I guess she was thinking and I...I couldn't say anything else. But she did finally speak, I think she was crying. She said, 'I hope you introduce me to the real you someday.' Then she hung up."

After the drinks we drove most of the way home in silence. Finally, Steve spoke. "I've had people leave or die around me. I'm never sure if I gave not enough, or maybe too much. Could I have saved them? Could I have spared myself the pain? What could I have done differently?"

I griped the steering wheel a little more tightly. "I guess we never know."

"We can only learn to live with our choices, and if we really think we made a mistake in the past, vow to do it differently next time."

My knuckles were red. "But can we change an old mistake?"

"No."

I wanted to slam on the brakes. Grab him and shake some sense into him. Who was he to say no!? How did he pretend to know? Did he think he had it all figured out!?

I saw the redness of my knuckles and wondered what good my anger was doing me. Somehow I lost grasp of it, and my anger became like the white line that trailed in the rearview mirror behind me.

"Do you want her back?" Steve's voice startled me.

I managed a weak "Yes."

"You should go for what you want." I knew Steve was looking at me, but I didn't dare return the gaze.

"Not to redo anything that's already been done," he went on. "But because you want it now. Be true to yourself. Don't go back to pay an old debt. Go back because it's what you want now!"

"But how will things be different?"

"Because it'll be what you want."

"But it was what I wanted all along!"

"Are you sure?"

"Yes!" Then a little doubt crept in. "Why, do you think what I want has changed?"

"I didn't know you then."

"I asked her to marry me, didn't I?"

"Why did you?"

"I don't know. Because it was the right thing to do. I knew it was right!" I exclaimed.

"It still doesn't mean you wanted to."

"Of course I wanted to! I wouldn't have asked her if I didn't want to!" I was aware that my voice was growing louder.

"Oh," was all he said. Then added, "Because I know that wants are the most powerful thing, more powerful than any laws. If a man wants to do something bad enough he'll break any law, and face any consequence. Nothing can stop someone who wants something bad enough."

With that I pulled up into his drive. Steve put a hand to the knob to open the door, but before opening it he turned back at me and asked, "Do you love her?"

When I made no immediate response he opened the door, and left.

I drove home in silence. The silence of my thoughts. Barely a whisper. Alone.

* * *

That night I dreamt I told Joan that I loved her. I woke in a cold sweat. I don't want to be alone. It was all I could think as I hugged my pillow, almost violently. I don't want to be alone.

I got up to fix myself a cup of strong coffee. I didn't want to sleep. I could almost hear Steve's voice saying, "You don't want to sleep...good! That narrows it down. Now what do you want?"

I'm afraid of being alone. Should I call Steve? No, that's silly. I can make it alone tonight, I'm just not sure I can make it the rest of my life. Alone. Forever. It sent chills down my spine.

Still, somewhere from the dark recesses of my brain his voice persisted, "What do you want?"

I don't want to be alone. No, but that's something I don't want. I could spend my life narrowing it down, finding all the things that I didn't want until one day—surprise!—this is what I want. By then I would probably be an old man, and die upon finally finding this evasive "what I want."

Was that what I wanted?

The coffee was finished. I poured a cup, trying not to think. But eventually I knew I must face that question, "what was it that what I wanted?"

To die?

Was it as simple as that?

All your problems go away when you no longer exist.

Somehow I bet if I were dead, being alone would lose its bite. To be free at last.

It would all be over.

No worries.

No cares.

No.

It is not what I want.

Somewhere I imagine a voice saying, "So the list narrows."

I cannot imagine being dead. More importantly, I don't want to be dead. I want to live.

"There, finally a want." The voice, still there, but not as harsh.

"In fact, I want to live more than I don't want to be alone!" My own voice startles me, but sounds good.

I could feel the power of the want. The power that had been missing for so long in my life. Missing, I'm sure, since I was a little boy.

"Wanting is okay," I told myself, soothing, over and over.

I could sense a barrier within. A wall, a line not to cross over. Somewhere, a long time ago, I had told myself it was not permissible to want. I had learned a hard lesson that I took with me into adulthood. Perhaps it had been a toy that I had wanted that my father wouldn't let me have. Perhaps it was my parents' love that I wanted more of— that I couldn't get. It could have been many of the things a young boy wants, then learns it's not all right. It's not polite to ask. Be a man. A man has no wants.

Where had it all started? Did it matter? I couldn't see what difference it could make; it only mattered that I was free to want now. I'm sure even Steve could agree with that.

But what was my own particular want that had been snuffed out as a young boy?

I curled up on the sofa, hot cup of coffee in my belly, smile on my face, and fell asleep.

But as I was drifting off, still the voice repeated, "So, what do you want?"

* * *

It must have been the caffeine, it didn't keep me from finding dreamland, it just turned my dreams into nightmares.

I saw faces. Haunting faces. Coming at me. From every side. They weren't just any faces. They were people I had known through the years. All distorted and misshapen, but I could recognize them. Each and every one. Faces from the past as well as the present. Faces I have long since forgotten, now they came back to me as horrible figures. Heads only, drifting through space, one by one, passing me from every angle. The eyes. Oh, they all watched me. Looking. Looking. Into my soul they saw. And one by one they nodded. They nodded and drifted passed, these horrible faces. Some smiled, an evil grin across their face. Some just looked. All nodded. They waited until I looked into their hideous eyes, and then they nodded.

It's like they had a secret that they weren't letting me in on.

They came forever. There was no end. They drifted one right after another and I knew there was no escape. Nowhere to hide. I could never run from those eyes, watching. Knowing.

I woke out of breath. I reached for a blanket to chase away the chill running down my spine.

My throat was dry. I gulped down the last few drops of the cold coffee on my night table.

I cleared my head, trying to erase the nightmare.

Why was it such a nightmare?

It made little sense, as many dreams do, in the waking hours.

But I could still feel the fear.

The fright was real.

I remember the faces. Were they really all that scary? I recognized them all. No dark strangers here. They hadn't all hurt me in one way or another, no, that wasn't it. It was everybody. Except...not everybody.

Who was missing? Maybe that was significant.

I again tried to picture the faces. I pushed past the fear and tried to concentrate.

Faces. Everywhere faces. Who was missing?

Joan? Yes, I definitely don't remember seeing her face.

So Joan was the key.

Key to what? What was this to prove? It was just a dream. But somehow I felt a need...no, a want...to decipher this dream. It seemed important.

Was it that everybody, except Joan had a potential to hurt me, and—coincidence—I chased her away?

Yes, could be. But I wasn't certain. Was this dream telling me to go running back to Joan in a fit of apologies? With that thought my stomach knotted up. No matter how I wanted to believe that's what it meant, it just didn't feel right.

But Joan's face wasn't in the dream, by now I was sure of it— which must be significant.

So who else was missing?

Steve.

I thought for a moment. No, he was there. Yes, I definitely remember Steve's accusing eyes drifting by.

I tried to think of others. I could only think of people as they drifted passed. I tried to clear my head from the dream so that I could think.

"What do you want?" the voice said.

"I want to figure this out," I told myself, thinking maybe my ears need to hear it.

Elise. Was she there?

How about Sally?

I tried to get the dream back to see if I could spot them, but it was cloudy, and I couldn't make out the faces.

How about Sue from work, or Jennifer?

But I hardly knew them!

Yet, many of the faces that had drifted by in that dream were people that I had only seen once, maybe twice.

How about Meg, or Sharon?

I could not control my hand. It was shaking. I could not make it stop.

From the darkened depths within, churning up from the core, an ignored leprous feeling, rising, rising up again to be confronted. To be feared.

All the faces had been men.

The feeling of terror consumed me; I let it wash over me, over, and away. I did not embrace it. I did not fight it.

Every last face was that of a man.

What did they want of me?

What did they know that I didn't?

I wanted to be like them all.

"What do you really want?" says the voice.

* * *

"I don't know how to say this." I paused. "I don't know if I want to say this." God, here come the wants again.

I had Steve's attention. He waited patiently. I guess I made it sound like an emergency, the way I called him up, asking if he could come over, "No," I corrected myself, "can I come over there, instead. Somehow I think it will be easier that way."

It was barely a day after my revelation. After my dream. It seemed like months. So much had happened in such a short time, but it had all happened inside. I felt so different. The world was still the world, and I was still me, only I felt like more of me. I felt like I had been a shadow, and now I was whole. No longer transparent.

"How are you feeling?" Steve asked, breaking the silence.

I looked at him. "Good," was all that I said, but I held his gaze.

"You look good." He leaned slightly forward. "To tell you the truth I was worried. The way you called me up. It sounded urgent."

I couldn't help smiling. Was urgent always bad?

Tilting his head slightly to one side he commented, "But you look relaxed."

"I don't think I'm feeling relaxed. I feel good, don't get me wrong, but I can't honestly say relaxed."

"You sound sure of it."

"Huh?"

"You sound like you know exactly how you feel." Steve leaned back in his chair. He shook his head. "I'm not used to that from you."

"I must have sounded pretty confused to you. I've been pretty messed up lately. I know you've had to listen to a lot of crap from me that maybe I should have saved for a psychiatrist but..."

"Don't talk like that!" he interrupted. "What are friends for?"

I almost wanted to cry. It just didn't sound good, for with all my heart—I knew that he meant it.

"And I'm glad," he said. "It is a good thing to know how you feel, I don't think you did in the past. I see that you are afraid, and more than that, I see how aware you are of that fact. It only makes you more you. I see such a difference in you today...it is...wonderful," spoke Steve in amazement, and the warmth of his smile made me think I had been a fool to think that I did not have the courage to go on with this.

"Well, I just want to thank you. You don't know how much you've done for me." I stopped, unsure of what to say, or more precisely, how to say it.

I fought the words out, "That's why I wanted to see you." Don't get cold feet now! "Since you've helped me so much, I thought it only right that I should tell you first."

I paused for a breath. *Just get it over with,* I thought. "I had a little revelation last night. Something I think I've known for a while. It just makes sense. It fits. I have been hiding it for, God, a long time now. I've been hiding it...mainly from myself. I don't know how it is possible, but while underneath I think I knew it, somehow I hid it from myself. At least I choose not to look too closely. I looked away and pretended that it wasn't so. Sometimes, when I was young, and it was harder to hide it from myself, I used to pray...literally pray to God, that it was not so!

"The older I got, the better I got, not at facing it, but hiding from it, until I really believed that it wasn't so. I really had myself fooled.

"Only, a part of me still knew, always knew, and would never deny it. It was always right there, under the surface, waiting. There were signs, but I continued to push them away.

"I was so afraid. Because it wasn't right. It wasn't good. But," I took a deep breath, "... it was me. And it hurt me every time I hid from it. A part of me died each time I chose to look the other way. As I sank deeper into the denial, my very being sank. Until I was no longer human."

I knew I was still hiding. Why couldn't I just come out and tell him? What was I so afraid of? Rejection. Disgust.

"You seem very human to me." Steve knew my pain. But how? How could Steve possibly know what I went through? Yet it was as obvious as the fear that knotted up my throat, he knew my pain. But would he be revolted by the reason for my pain?

"I am human, because I chose to hide no longer. I know I can, or will, never hide it from myself again—for it is who I am." My breath came more quickly now. "But I no longer want to hide from the outside world, either, I know that that also is a part of my pain."

"It's not easy." I know at this point I was pleading. "But I need to be able to say it, out loud, and not care who hears."

"Just say it." I heard Steve's words, but again found it difficult to look at him.

I felt ashamed.

Here goes. And while looking at a particularly interesting spot on the carpet I said, "I'm gay."

Steve made no response.

Is he shocked? Or did he already know? Surely if anyone had it figured out it was Steve. The silence was killing me. The clock ticked off seconds, while days of thoughts surged through my head.

"Did you know?" I finally had to ask..

"No," he lied. It was a lie, wasn't it? Surely he had already guessed, or at least had some idea. But maybe he didn't.

Then, a thought occurred to me. "You're not...?"

"No, I'm not." Finally a smile came to his lips.

I fell back in my chair. A feeling of relief washed over me. I knew, and now Steve knew. What did he think of me? I honestly didn't care. I thought I was all right, and for the first time in my life, that was all that mattered.

Steve rose from his chair. Oh well, I chased him away. But I still felt better having told him. Even if my "little secret" meant chasing others away, at least now I could face myself.

But he came over to me.

He hugged me.

Then, when our grip finally loosened, at arm's length, looking into my eyes, he said, "You are wonderful. And God," tears were streaming down his face, "so brave!"

I cried.

PART G

DROWNING

The beer tasted bad.

The brand, one of my preferred, was fine; the concept, drowning sorrows, was plausible; the setting, a dark and dingy bar, was good; the time, the middle of an ordinary day, was right.

Yet, somehow the beer just tasted bad. I forced each sip down; hoping the introduction of the sour taste into my mouth would make the bitterness in the pit of my stomach somehow lessen.

Trying to drink oneself into bliss, or AA, whichever came first, was almost impossible when one was so conscience of each and every sip.

Alcohol only accomplished weakening my defenses, lessening the shell I had built up around myself. Alcohol let the pain in. It cut through the buffer zone I had worked long and hard to build up. The pain was suddenly made real, and unlike a true drunk, I always remember the pain upon awakening the next morning. The hangovers were all huge, but never covered the remembrance of the pain from the night before. It seemed unfair that I should remember little of the fun of getting drunk but most of the pain.

With each gulp I felt isolation wash over me like a whirlpool of great fury. It washed the pain, not away, but up from the depths where they had lain for years, silent, festering, forever growing and mutating, yet undisturbed and overlooked. I hid from the pain just as it seemed to be hiding from me. My fear of the pain was great. And the greater my denial of the pain, the more the fear grew, because I knew that my fear also grew. Deep...waiting.

The beer was the catalyst in the overturning of the stone. I so feared what lay beneath that I turned that fear toward the beer, so that with every drink I imagined drowning. Drowning in the depths of my own garbage, buried, yet still unable to force my eyes to close.

At last I could take no more, face no more. I laid a twenty on the counter and made my way towards the door. The place was almost empty, so I'm sure that the few patrons, along with the bartender, noticed my departure. Quick, silent departures were always the best— avoid the awkwardness and uncomfortability of casual, superficial good-byes.

Before I reached the door, there was a knock. I looked around to see if anyone else had heard it before opening it, but no one seemed to be paying attention.

I was a little curious to see who was on the other side of the door. What type of creature knocks before entering a bar?

It was still light outside and as I opened the door the contrast between the dark and dingy interior and the cloudlessness of the outside afternoon hurt my eyes. I looked through squinted eyes to a lone figure standing in this bright, outside, foreign world.

The sun was behind him, outlining his frame, giving him a kind of glow that nonetheless blurred his features.

"Hello," he said.

I said nothing. I may have even taken a step back, for his presence seemed overwhelming. His voice was now softer as he asked, "Is something wrong?"

"I just..." I heard my voice stammering, as if it had been gone for years. "I just...feel lost."

"Ha! That makes two of us." He took a step to the side and with the sun no longer directly behind him, I saw him more clearly. He was just a man. Ordinary. "To think I came looking for directions!"

I stepped out into his world and closed the door behind me.

"Perhaps someone in there..." He pointed toward the door as I closed it.

"I am more mentally lost than geographically. What did you need to find?" I asked.

"Just a lost soul looking to give directions," he laughed. His laugh was free and easy, and his smile genuine.

"Somehow when we're lost, it makes it more bearable to know that others are lost too."

"Or alone..." His eyes penetrated.

My head went swirling. I felt like a frightened child who had hid too well in a game of hide-n-seek, to be found, hours later, by a parent, after the rest of the children have long gone.

"We're never really lost when someone else is around." He smiled.

"Can't we both be lost?"

"Isn't the whole world lost."

"You mean 'not on the right path'?" I questioned.

"Right path, or any path?"

"Yes." I understood. "Not moving...wandering."

"The trouble is, that up close, wandering looks like movement. It's only from a more distant and objective perspective that it is seen to be what it truly is...wandering."

"But you have a destination in mind, so you can ask me for directions. How about when we don't know where we want to go?"

"Just as I can ask for directions, I can as easily ask for a destination."

"From God?"

"From you," yet he nodded. "Inside." He pointed toward my chest.

In a syrupy voice I stated, "All the answers are within."

He only nodded, my sarcasm going unnoticed. He seemed so smart, yet so naïve.

"You seem to pick up on the little, meaningless things, yet when something is very obvious you totally ignore it!" I confronted him.

"Perhaps it is the obvious things that are meaningless."

"The world is a mystery!" I laughed.

"Only to shrouded eyes."

"I don't understand..."

"If your world is dark, don't curse the light."

"Should I curse the dark?"

"Neither is effective."

"Damn, are you saying I shouldn't curse?"

"One who invites darkness can just as easily invite light, and light is the illumination of the darkness."

"All I have to do is turn on a switch?"

"Even easier than that. The light is always there, but for you to see it."

"Even at night?"

"Even in the darkest conditions don't your eyes eventually become adjusted to the dark?"

"To see a little. Total darkness becomes at best— shadows...outlines, but we're talking light. Illumination!" I exclaimed.

"It takes light to see. If you can see anything in what you call 'total darkness' there must be some light there. Perhaps you are just not adjusted to looking for it. Light, truly, is everywhere."

We walked along.

"Is there light where you're going?" I asked.

"If I but choose to see it."

"Which is?"

"Huh?" He stopped in his tracks and turned to me with a puzzled look on his face.

"Where are you headed?"

"Oh." He laughed. "Here's the address."

I took the tattered and torn piece of paper from him. 1496 Eastham Dr. was scrawled out in neat letters.

"Ha!" It was my turn to laugh. "I know where that is."

"A friend of yours?"

"An acquaintance...old friend." I muttered. It seems I had lost all my friends. They blamed it on my drinking, but I know that it was just because I am an asshole. Pure and simple, people didn't like me because I'm not very likable.

"Are we far?" he asked, breaking my muttled thoughts.

"Huh." It was my turn to be confused, because for some time now it seems it was I who was following him.

"1496 Eastham. Is it far?"

"Oh. Ha! It just so happens our wandering has been in the right direction. It's right around the next corner."

We walked the rest of the way in silence. I pointed the house out to him.

He held out his hand. "Steve."

It took me a second to realize he had just told me something I didn't know, his name. I shook his hand and replied, "My name's Gerry."

"Should I say hi to Albert for you?" he said while pointing to the house.

"Nah, I don't think it would be a good idea."

"Well, I'll at least put in a kind word for you."

His grip was warm and friendly, somehow it was hard to let go.

Although I haven't seen him since, I think about a lot of the things he said that day. But the thing I find myself thinking about mostly was the last thing he said to me.

With a sparkle in his eye, he looked through me and without cringing he said, "Light. It can illuminate and thus eliminate pain, also. Peace."

GRIP

Closing the door, I couldn't help but laugh. David was full of surprises.

But maybe it shouldn't have been such a surprise. Sometimes fear of the consequences of reality makes someone try to disguise that reality by acting the opposite of their feelings. I once ran into Elise at the tennis club when Dave wasn't around. We had a drink at the bar together.

I had brought up the subject of David. "How long have you known David?"

"Oh." Elise stopped, pursing her lips while she thought. "I really only know him through his wife...er, ex-wife. I've known her for years."

"Oh, I'm surprised David still talks to you!" I laughed.

"David is...interesting," she relayed.

"How so?"

"Well, out of all Joan's friends I think I'm the only one who could get along with him."

"He seems like a nice enough guy." I was genuinely surprised.

"Sure you would say that—you're a man." She was quick to counter. "The way he comes on to females...but I know better."

"Well, I hope he doesn't come on to you."

"Oh, he comes on to all females. Even though Joan and I are close friends that doesn't stop him. But I have an advantage, I can see through him, for through Joan I definitely know he's all talk and no action."

"Oh." Suddenly she turned beat red. "I shouldn't have told you that. I don't know what got over me...I don't usually gossip."

"Don't worry about it," I reassured her.

"It's just...you're so easy to talk to." A cute smile crept to her lips.

Elise was quite a girl.

Now I can see how this conversation was significant and possibly would have saved me the embarrassment of total shock when David did let me in on his secret. I only should have paid more attention to her words instead of her cute smile. She was a quiet girl, but I had the feeling that when she did talk it was noteworthy.

David had left, almost in a hurry. It was like he was anxious to start anew.

Vaguely I wondered what his revelation would mean to our friendship. I couldn't see where it would have any negative bearing, but one never knew.

He had thanked me. What did I do?

I guess I had been there when he needed someone, just to talk, just to listen.

I had been there for David. Like I wasn't there for Liz? Liz was dead, and David is gay. Man, what an effect I have on people.

Why did David choose to tell me first? True, I am his friend—but how about his wife?

Telling his wife might not be too easy of a task. I wonder if she already knew? Was that why she left him? Did she suspect? Just from what Elise had said, Joan seemed to know that something was funny. All talk. No action? No wonder...

Why didn't I suspect? I guess that's not usually something one looks for in someone. I think that David thought I knew before he did. But he floored me. It took me totally by surprise. If I were to list fifty reasons why David seemed to have an urgent need to see me, and what he wanted to tell me, being gay wouldn't even have made the list.

Why did he tell me first? Does he know something that I am refusing to see? Why did being around me make it safe to— "remember"? Am I fooling myself just like David had been?

No, David was just my friend. It was safest to tell me first.

Sometimes I make things more complicated than they need be.

Somehow I couldn't help thinking of Liz. I was happy for David, yet...it was fleeting. Liz dominated my thoughts. Why I choose to focus on death rather than enlightenment is beyond me.

FLEX

Dave Armaun. Yes, I did remember him.

James must be a fool. First; to turn down a VP position, second; to recommend Dave Armaun for it.

James was a good man, a fool—but nonetheless a good man. A family man. Putting family before job opportunity. I didn't like it, I couldn't understand it, yet somehow I admired it. Maybe admire was too strong a word...

The fool. Sure, accepting the position would mean moving here, uprooting his family, losing friends, and disclaiming his belief in God. Well, why not? That's the way James made it sound!

Atlanta was about as far from Hell as you could get. I told him that. I don't think he believed me. I'm not sure why he couldn't have at least given it a try. Come down for a month to see if you like it, no strings attached, then send for the family once you've settled in.

The thing that showed James to be a real fool was his recommendation of Dave Armaun for the position.

Sure, it was not unlike me to skyrocket an employee through the ranks, if he showed the character and I felt the inkling to do so. For I place great importance in what I call "personal intuition." And no one else's "personal intuition" mattered but mine. After all, I own the company. If I want to be petty or unfair, it is my right. And I didn't get this successful by being wrong very often.

Dave Armaun? A VP? I had met him before. I don't pretend to know him well. I'd only met him once, and it was at a party, which is not the best of circumstances to form an opinion on somebody. But actually, that is usually all I need for my "personal intuition" to kick in.

And I remember this Dave Armaun. He came across as a dark

fellow. Closed. Muddled thoughts. A vice president of mine has to be a clear thinker, a forthright man. I have to be able to trust him with my last dollar. My impression of Dave Armaun is that I wouldn't trust him to walk my dog.

James assured me that Dave Armaun was a good man. The right man. But only my "personal intuition" mattered. I wouldn't have even granted an interview with Mr. Armaun if there weren't some facts to back up James' thoughts on the matter.

The evidence shows that this Dave Armaun character has been a shooting star as of late. The things he has done over the last few months have been very impressive. So where was he the first five years with the corporation? James says it's like he's had some kind of great awakening. But what good is that if he decides to go back to sleep tomorrow?

No, James' feelings and statistics aren't enough. Statistics can be deceiving, they rise and they fall—it's too easy to just notice the high points and forget the crashes. I go more by the averages. Average out what Mr. Armaun has done since he's been with us, and the impressiveness of the last few months fades below mediocrity. I don't need a flash in the pan for a VP.

I will interview Mr. Armaun for the position, but only because James highly recommends it, and his recent work warrants it. But I know the outcome of the interview before he walks through my door.

The interview was over an hour and a half long. I had to cancel two other appointments I had scheduled.

I found David to be a man whom I had never met. I remember meeting him, and my memory is usually excellent. And he says we had met before. His recollections, of our original meeting and that party, differ from mine in only the most minuet details. Yet, deep down I know that this is not the same man. People do not change this much!

"Welcome to the Vice Presidency of Couplex Incorporated, David."

"Thank you, sir." His handshake was firm and warm.

I'm not too big a man to admit that I can be wrong. But my personal intuition is never wrong. It can change, but it is never wrong.

PART H

ESCAPING

Shopping. With the excitement of buying on one's mind, sometimes little things go unnoticed. Small things, like a dark figure following from behind—sizing up his intended victim, are overlooked.

A swinging purse dead ahead, ripe for the picking. A man moves ahead, only focused on the sight of the purse, dangling from the woman's fingertips in front of him. She, only thinking of her next purchases; Him, only thinking of the purse and his escape route.

Her moving forward. Him, behind, but slowly gaining.

The two meet. The purse is tugged effortlessly from her grasp. She stops abruptly, too startled to move or scream. When she does finally find her voice the dark figure has already disappeared from her sight.

She futilely runs off in the direction that he had fled yelling, "Stop! Thief! He has my purse!"

She runs, knowing she is no match for his speed, but, not knowing what else to do, she continues her pursuit for a short while.

With tears welling up in her eyes, she is just about to give up, when she notices a commotion up ahead. Out of breath, she reaches the small crowd. In the center she sees a man holding her purse. As she steps forward she notices it is not the man who stole it. She stops short of the man, catching her breath, trying to size up the situation— when the man now with her purse catches her eye, and asks, "Is this your purse?"

Stepping forward with one last deep breath she speaks up, "Yes!

It's mine!"

"I sort of figured." The stranger smiles. He hands it back to her with no further questions.

But she is a little puzzled. She makes sure she had her purse, then she asks, "Where's the man who stole it?"

"Gone," is the stranger's simple reply.

"He got away?"

"You could say that."

The crowd was showing no signs of dissipating. The drama didn't quite seem over.

The lady stands in disbelief, staring accusingly at the stranger. "You let him go, didn't you?"

"Yes, I did."

"On purpose!"

"He won't do it again."

"How do you know!?"

"Because he said so."

"And you believed him!?"

"Everything is still in your purse, he didn't have time to go through it."

"That's not the point!"

"Revenge serves no purpose."

"Asshole! Now there is a criminal still on the streets." She storms away in a foul mood.

The stranger stands before the crowd, wanting to say something, to explain; he knows that there are a few there who already understand, but the majority were like the lady.

The stranger is afraid, not used to speaking to more than a few people, but words come from his lips. Most grow bored quickly and, seeing the action is over, leave. But a few stay behind to listen to his explanations, and talk with him afterward.

CHAPTER IV

HELP

"Steve, how do you feel?"

"About?"

"Liz. Dave."

"I'm sorry for Liz. I'm happy for Dave."

"Are you really?"

"Do you think it might be the opposite?"

"I'm not sure." He looked at me.

I thought about it. Liz was no longer suffering. She was free. Did I somehow envy her? I didn't think so, but maybe the psychiatrist saw something that I didn't.

And David. Was he, in affect, dead? Out of town. Out of my life. Only an occasional awkward phone call. He had made it. He was a success in the real world. He was just no longer in my world.

Liz had chosen to escape, David had chosen to join. Each found their way out. Away—from me.

I'm sure that now Liz was successful in her "world," just as David was in his. It didn't matter which I considered more important, just that each had, I was somehow sure, found their way out.

Each had left.

"How do you feel?" he repeated.

I thought for only a moment before answering, "Alone."

"Don't you have other friends?"

"I guess."

When I said nothing more he thoughtfully said, "You didn't really know the girl, Liz, for too long, or very well—you say. Yet, I sense that she touched you, had a deep effect on you. You connected at a level that we can only guess at. And I would suggest that you must have had the same effect on her. And you knew her for a very short time, really didn't know much about her. There was just that...connection."

I had to agree. "Yes, I have to admit that on one level I did feel very connected to her. But that is not uncommon. I mean, if I take the time to stop and talk to almost anyone I will feel a connection to him or her. I believe that there's a common link between everyone, it's just that most people don't see it, or look for it. With Liz I could feel her pain and her fright, which I know that I share with her. But I don't keep mine as visible as she...did."

I had to swallow. "I had to admire how up front and honest she was. She was so...real!"

"But then in many ways she made me unsettled. Maybe it was partly out of envy, because I knew that there were many things about her that I could not get a grasp on myself. She had so much nervous energy. I felt there was nothing I could do."

"Do?" questioned the doctor.

"To calm her," I explained. "Calming, or making people or situations comfortable seems almost to be a gift of mine. But she was different."

I tried to sit up straighter in the chair but I still felt as if I were slouching, and soon I would eventually melt into the very fabric of the chair. "Having no effect on her was almost...repulsive. It took me totally out of my context."

"The trouble is...now I wonder...if I did have an effect on her! And it was negative. And my 'effect' helped her. Helped her to commit suicide!" I spat.

"Do you really think you have that much control over people?" asked Dr. Rossintaul.

"No," I stated. "But I feel..."

I fell silent.

"And Dave..." he continued, just to stop the silence, stop me from retreating, "you knew him a little longer, but in actuality only for a short time, also. Do you feel responsible for him?"

"It's so maddening! Maybe I push them away and out of my life. Only then can they change and grow. Maybe I only hold people back, and the only effect I can have on anyone is to get out of their life."

The doctor nodded, but said, "Liz and Dave took a look at themselves, and neither liked what they saw. Each had their own way of handling their situation."

Dr. Rossintaul looked directly at me and I felt a shiver run down my spine as he said, "If all you do is make people look at themselves, what a wondrous gift that is!"

Then the doctor added, "But you are not responsible for other people's actions."

"It's more like a weight," I reasoned. "I don't even know it's there, until the other person is gone and I am left holding it...alone."

That got a raised eyebrow from the doctor, but from his mouth came the words, "We grow up with people. We grow old with people. Yet, seldom do we really know them. What you had with these two people, some spend a lifetime searching for. A closeness that defies time. Time is irrelevant; it's only the depth of feeling that can bring two people close. You can grow accustomed to someone, but it is much more difficult to grow close to them. Just as I'm sure that David was accustomed to his wife—but I would not call it close."

But instead of David and his ex-wife, I thought of Liz, saying, "Close enough to share one's innermost secretes, and close enough to give up when being rejected by this person."

The Doc was still talking, "Closeness bares an obligation, perhaps that is why so few choose to let another human in." He then asked, "Did you chose to let them in?"

"Yes..." Did I know how not to?

It was helping. I was really taking a good look at myself for the first time. I had been seeing a psychiatrist for about eight months, every other week, and it was helping.

His name was Jack. Dr. Jack Rossintaul, but I called him Jack. Right from the start I had simply called him Jack. I'm not sure he approved. I know that all his patients probably eventually called him by his first name, but only after he had told them to do so. Giving permission to be informal leads to a certain proper trust. But right from the start, I took the liberty of calling him by his first name; I had never called him Dr. Rossintaul. Taking that informality without first getting permission gnaws at the very meat of the doctor/patient relationship. Just a little rock of the boat to keep things interesting. Yes, I've always been a passive troublemaker.

At first I think that it threw him a little, but by now I'm sure he doesn't even think about it.

I don't take everything he says as gospel. I think he knows this, and I think it helps our interaction, and my progress. When what one says is taken too seriously, it leads to one not wanting to say anything.

The good Doctor Jack doesn't just sit back and say, "What do you think about that?" or "What do you think that it means?" He gives his opinions, and that makes me more free to give mine.

For example, he might suggest that a dream might mean this; then I will say that I think it has more to do with that. When he makes a suggestion I always stop to think about it, but it doesn't keep me from considering other possibilities.

"The possibilities are endless," he will often say. "So what is the reality?"

I often find that reality changes from day to day. The only constant is change.

"Change will always get you four quarters for a buck," is another of Jack's little sayings.

Sometimes I think I go to Jack more for his sense of humor than his understanding and compassion. Jack definitely has a weird way of coming across, but somehow I find myself back in his chair. And his unorthodox ways help me to see things faster and more clearly.

"Words of the wise are lost on the unwise. And do wise men really need to hear the words? What for, they're already wise?"

"Is that a fancy way of saying 'go figure it out for yourself'?" I ask.

"To keep a secret is to bring about its end."

"Ah, life without secrets. Harmony and peace."

"Peace and harmony are the secret."

"Are you sure you're a psychiatrist, and not a philosopher?"

Sometimes the bulk of our sessions is this type of back and forth banter. Sometimes it goes nowhere, and other times it loosens me up for some pretty deep soul-searching.

Sometimes you need to laugh as well as cry. Sometimes it's only laughter that can make it safe enough for the tears to come out. Lately I laugh and cry often.

* * *

MORE SESSIONS

A bit of this and that
THE PROTECTION OF SOLITUDE

"You want to be alone?"

"At the moment?" I smile.

"You know what I mean." Damn him, Jack was in one of his serious moods.

"No, I don't want to be alone."

"So you have made another friend?"

"Sort of."

"Oh, I see...a distant acquaintance."

"I guess you could call it that."

"And it's your choice to keep it that way?"

"Yes."

"Hmm."

"Do you doubt my word?"

"No. I just want convincing," Jack states matter-of-factly.

"Convincing?"

"Yes. Convince me on how much you don't want to get close to this person."

"She..." realizing I had jumped in too quickly, without knowing what to say, I stopped in thought. She was...What was she?

"Well?" prodded the good doctor.

I figured I would start with her name. "Elise." That was safe.

"Unusual name. Pretty, yet somehow mysterious." As doctor Jack talked my mind raced...

Yes, she was pretty! I could spend a lifetime researching the mystery of her smile. It was there so freely, shining in glory, yet, somehow never the same. It was ever changing, from a warm "how are you" greeting, to a melancholy, wistful hint of a smile. The only thing that remained consistent was its genuineness, and my desire to see it. The fact that I could make that smile come out at times had the same effect on me as if I could make the sun come out from behind the clouds.

So why do I do so many rain dances?

"So why do you want to keep her far away?" Jack interrupted my train of thought with his persistence.

Answering both his, and my question, I relayed, "To protect her."

"Do you really think that she needs protection from you?"

"I'm not sure."

"You're not a bad guy."

"That's a relative term."

"How so?"

"Isn't everyone worse than their ideal?"

"True, thus the desire to improve, to grow."

"I don't want any harm to come to her."

"Surely you're fooling everyone, including me, if you turn out to be a violent man."

"That's not what I mean." My voice is weak.

"Someone else will hurt her? What's that to do with you?"

"Not someone. Nature."

"Your mother wasn't struck by lightning."

"Leave my mother out of it." I wanted to get angry, I wanted to yell at him, but I only felt weak. I wanted to leave, but I knew that my legs were too weak for me to stand, just as my voice was too weak to shout. "It has nothing to do with my mother."

"Well, if that's too uncomfortable, then just think of Liz...or Steve. How about Elise?"

I finally managed a frail yell between my hands that were cupped in front of my face. Mom! Liz! Steve! Was it all the same?

Elise, protect yourself!

"It's all the same. It will happen to Elise. She needs protection." I managed to project some of my feelings.

"Perhaps it is you who needs the protection," said Jack, making my head spin all the more. "Perhaps this is what you will learn here."

"Huh?"

"You have no control over the lives of loved ones, the choice of when to leave is theirs, and God's. Maybe all you need to learn is acceptance."

* * *

CLIFFS AND FEARS

"What you seem to be saying, is that you...consider death, and someone moving on—changing their direction, to be similar?" It sounded like a trap, but Jack wouldn't do that to me, he was about as up front as a breast reduction surgeon.

"In a way I do see death as simply moving on." I'm sure he was wondering why I was smiling, probably summed it up to some dark childhood event.

"So abandonment and death are simply about moving on?"

"I guess."

"Doesn't that make you angry?"

"I don't know if anger is the correct word."

"What is a better word?" the doctor prodded.

"There's a certain...hopelessness involved."

"How so?"

"If someone chooses to leave, or chooses to have you be a smaller part of their life, or if someone dies, there is very little you can do about it."

"So the only way to have control over your life is to unplug from as many of these unknown variables as possible?"

"I guess there is a certain safety in becoming a hermit."

"Is that where you're headed?"

"I know that I haven't been involved in much other than work lately, but I...don't know."

"And if you did know?"

"Every curve in a winding road is potential disaster. And if you took a snapshot along that road, you would surely see a car about to go off a cliff. Thank God for steering wheels."

"So what is your steering wheel?"

I thought about it for a moment, then answered honestly, "Maybe I haven't found it yet."

"How close to the edge are you going to get?"

"The best view is from the edge."

"What are you trying to see?"

"Myself—no, God."

"You don't sound sure."

"If I could just get a closer look perhaps I'd be sure."

"Closer to you, or to God?"

"Hmm." I thought about it but made no response.

"Maybe you're just trying to see what feeling vulnerable is like."

"Huh?" As usual, I was at my articulate best when I was confused.

"I'm not sure you've ever felt vulnerable before. Accepting someone else's vulnerability is one thing, but being vulnerable yourself is entirely something else."

Jack walked from one end of the room to the other. He ran his fingers across the top of some books on his bookshelf. Looking for dust, or did he just like the feel of books? Books—heavy, seemingly permanent, solid. Was Jack having as much trouble getting a grasp on me as I was?

"Your spirituality and your humanity seem so...separate." Jack's voice was soft, and from across the room I had to concentrate a little more to hear his words. "Maybe you could learn to bridge that gap.

"To be whole," I whispered. Sometimes I think I would rather be a hole, so you could fill me with dirt and forget about me.

"So what can you do to better yourself and the world?" Jack asked.

"Well, let's see, I meditate every morning and I recycle."

Jack was not laughing, or joking. "Maybe you just need to reach out. Step out of yourself."

"I don't want to change."

"Change or grow?"

"Well..."

"You wouldn't be here if you didn't want to grow. And with growth there's change. And there's change in learning, whether it's learning facts, or learning to cope."

"Or being vulnerable."

"It would be a change for you."

"But I always feel vulnerable."

"It's true that you fear it, and that's why you attempt to keep it away. Pushing, always pushing and running from it, but this actually only leaves you in a constant vulnerable state without you really feeling it, or accepting it. Your choice is to never feel vulnerable, which is an impossible state, and thus paradoxically you must always feel vulnerable. It's all about acceptance and choice."

"I'm vulnerable with you," I offered.

"It's a start. But you need to try it on someone you're not paying."

"Semantics, if I were having sexual problems, I wonder if he'd feel the same way about me going to a prostitute?" I whispered, glade he didn't hear.

"How about Elise?" Jack was back from across the room, back to reality, or was it from reality, to bring me back to it?

I made no response, and he continued, "When's the last time you've seen her."

"Well, I really haven't run into her in quite a while."

"Run into her? That sounds powerless."

"I'm not exactly feeling dynamic, presently."

"You could call her."

"I wouldn't know what to say."

"What would you like to say?"

"I would...just like to hear her voice."

"Could you tell her that?"

I thought about that. I pictured it. I saw a hundred scenarios in my head, but I didn't say a word.

Finally he broke the silence by saying, "What if it wasn't for the fear that's holding you back?"

* * *

FEELING NEEDED

"Yes, I used to get out a lot."

"Parties? Bars?"

"Sometimes. But mostly I just like walking, meeting people."

"Isn't that dangerous?"

"No."

"There are a lot of sick people out there."

"What sickness doesn't long to be cured?"

"And you have the cure?"

"No, but they do."

"Huh?"

"No offense, doctor, but I believe that everyone cures themselves."

"Ha! None taken." Dr. Jack laughed. "But if you believe that I can do no good for you, then why are you here?"

"Oh, I didn't say that others couldn't help. Sometimes listening...caring...is of great help, but ultimately the real cure comes from the patient."

"So if you know this, why don't you cure yourself?"

"Because sometimes one needs a smart-aleck doctor to be

reminded of it."

* * *

EMOTIONAL GUIDE

"Silence versus noise?"

"I prefer silence."

"But doesn't noise sometimes block out the inner demons?"

"Quite the contrary, I believe that in silence we hear our own inner voice, or God."

"For the lack of a better word...?" snickered Jack.

"Words mean different things to different people."

The doctor sat back, and after a moment he asked, "What does evil mean to you?"

"Evil is misguided emotions."

"You answered very fast!"

"I've thought about it before."

"Is that because sometimes you feel evil?"

"I would say it's more because it's always seemed such a strange concept to me."

"So you have no evilness in you?"

"I'm sure that I have done things that others have seen as evil."

"But you haven't felt evil?"

"No. I have had strong emotions that have turned negative, but I don't see it as evil, just misguided."

"Aren't emotions just a way of expressing both good and evil?"

"I think that when someone is either suppressing an emotion, or afraid of it, that is when we see behavior that we term evil."

"So you think it is not good to express emotions?"

"Quite the contrary, I said the suppression of emotions!"

"As in suppressed anger that leads to rage?"

"Exactly."

"So then rage is evil?"

"No." I thought for a moment. "Rage is like a bomb, pent up energy that is released all at once; it, as is a bomb, is neither good nor evil, yet it surely can be used in evil ways."

"So is the one who uses this 'bomb' in evil ways, himself evil?"

"I like to think of it as misguided."

"As you've said, words mean different things to different people."

* * *

PARTYING FOOL

"You need to get out more."

"Yes."

"How often you have said it."

"Yes."

"What are you going to do about it?"

"I'm not sure."

"You are a people person. You have much to offer...and maybe, much to experience. If you want." He looked at me, shaking his head, and said, "So what are you going to do about it? And don't tell me that walking around, meeting an occasional stranger, saying a couple words to them and moving on is your way of giving, or of experiencing life."

"Aren't they one in the same?"

"What?"

"Giving of oneself, and experiencing life?"

"I'm not sure. Sometimes experiencing life can be about witnessing, or even taking."

"As in, to take a breath?"

"Yes!" laughed the doc, "but I'm sure that you would see yourself as giving—carbon dioxide!"

* * *

At the end of this particular session he handed me one of his cards with an address scrawled on the back.

"Show up here. It's a party. Dress formally. There will be many interesting people to meet. Consider it your first home work assignment."

Towards the end of the next session he asked me about the party. "Did you go?"

"Yeah. I was surprised you weren't there."

He shrugged his shoulders.

"There were a lot of nice people there."

"So you had a good time?"

"Yes. A little too fancy for me, though."

"Stuffy, eh?"

"I guess you could say that."

"It's not the people, it's the atmosphere. It's part of human nature to fit into one's surroundings. Most people will not only act differently, but talk about different things when they are at a fast food restaurant as opposed to a fancy restaurant."

"Peer pressure?"

"Maybe more like suppression. Did you ever wonder how man would behave if no one was around, judging, watching, with certain expectations."

"It would be bliss."

"Bliss can mean different things to different people."

"If a rose went by any other name, wouldn't it be as sweet?"

"It depends on which nose is doing the smelling." He paused, as if hesitant to go on. Finally he said, "You might think that those people at the party are stuffy, but you haven't seen them loosen up. I should invite you to one of their 'other' parties."

"Hmm," he said after a moment's contemplation. "I'm not sure you could handle it though."

I looked at him, trying to gauge whether he was serious. "Really?" was all I said.

"Those calm, proper folks can definitely get weird."

"Weird?"

"You might say dark."

I tried to figure out what he meant by dark.

He said, "You want to go to one?"

"Maybe I'm not ready for it."

"No," he agreed with a nod.

* * *

THE PATH MOST STRANGE

"You like to meet people, how would you categorize the various people you come across?"

"I'm not sure what you mean?"

"You know...strangers."

"I try not to think of myself as a stranger?"

"Huh?"

"People are strange, when you're a stranger."

"Ah, a 'Doors' philosopher. If Eric Clapton is God, then maybe Jim Morrison is Christ?"

The look I gave, from his response to it, I guess said it all. For he said, "Is it that absurd?"

"I certainly hope so!" I couldn't help shuttering just a bit.

"Why?"

"They had their...problems."

"And Jesus had none?"

"I guess it's not the problems that separate us, it's the way we handle them."

"Perhaps some people just don't know how, and that's what gets them into trouble. Do you have a sure fire way to handle your troubles, or foul moods."

"If I did would I be here?"

"I'm not sure."

I ignored his innuendo as I thought of something and relayed it to him. "I remember I was in a very foul mood once, I felt trapped. Claustrophobic—I was inside during a blizzard, with no way to get out, nor anywhere to go to if I could get out. When I could take no more of the four walls, I bundled up and went outside. Yet, it seemed I didn't bundle up enough, for the moment I stepped out—I was freezing. The snow was blowing around me in swirls and, I swear, I could not see more than five feet in front of me. My teeth were chattering, yet I had all this pent-up energy and I dreaded going back to my familiar four walls. I stood there; it seemed, for the longest time, slowly turning into a snowman, when an almost involuntary action caused me to pick up a snow shovel. I went out to the front sidewalk and furiously started shoveling."

"I bet you were no longer cold?" Dr. Jack interjected.

I thought about that for a moment. "Maybe the coldness did leave me first, I had always thought it was my mood that changed first.

"Anyway, I was trying to focus only on the physical act of shoveling, trying to get lost in a situation, in a world that I already felt lost in. As my arms grew heavy, I'm not sure my mood was growing light.

"Suddenly there was someone else there! With the snow coming down so heavily, I didn't see her until she was right on top of me. I think she was as startled as I was. I think she said something to the effect that I was crazy. I looked to the piles of snow I had made along the edges of the sidewalk, and wondered what I was trying to bury. For a split second, I had to agree with her, but then when I looked at this fellow snowman, legs probably weary from trudging through deep piles of snow, I think, for the first time, I looked to the path I had created, and realized that for a moment her burden would be less. Here was another lost soul, I told myself. I then told her I that I had shoveled for her. I don't remember her saying anything; I just remember a smile. She walked ahead on the path that I had created for her. She taught me. I believed it, as she did, that this path was for her. She taught me to trust. Sometimes, things don't always turn out the way they're headed when we start. But there is a reason.

"I think of Liz. And I think of David. I know there is reason to it all. I may not understand it now, but hopefully someday it will be clear."

* * *

ELISE SAY YOU TRIED

"You talk about Elise as if she's dead or moved on to a different plane of existence."

"Like Liz or David?"

"Is that how it feels?"

"No."

"You sound sure..." Doubt hung over his voice.

"I am."

"Oh?"

"For now."

"And in the future?"

"That's what it is! I just don't want it to end with her like those other two scenarios."

"And why should it?"

"Doesn't death come in threes?"

"Third time's a charm."

"Maybe..."

"It all depends on how you look at it. Don't you think I've seen the gamete of situations? I've seen people stuck because their brand of shampoo has been discontinued. Then I've seen people who go on better with the loss of a child. We are mere mortals; there are always many, many reasons to stop living. We can always find fear. It is up to us as individuals whether we embrace it or look past it."

"But isn't there always a safety period? A time to regroup?"

"Yes, and that is very healthy. But at some point it becomes stagnant, or maybe I should say comfortable. And sometimes when we wait, past that critical point we can forever go into a regroup mode, and it becomes harder and harder to get back into the real world."

"Are you," swallow, swallow, "telling me that you think I'm ready?"

"What do you think?"

"Watch it! You starting to sound like a shrink!"

"It's my job and I won't deny it!"

"Oh thy sweet curse of denial."

"It only tastes sweet when you're fooling others and yourself."

There was a long pause. I broke the silence with a one-word question, "Elise?"

He simply was nodding, finally he said, "Do you want to rehearse anything?"

PART I

THIEF

I think of myself differently. It sounds simple. It sounds stupid. But with my thoughts I have changed myself. It all started as a seed, planted by a stranger.

It wasn't that long ago, but it seems as if it's from another lifetime. I didn't like myself, then. But I was what I was, and more importantly I knew what I was. I knew how to act. I guess that in some respect I felt it was my role. Expected by me, and supported by the outside world.

I was a thief. I stole. It was not based on need, it was more based on opportunity. If something was obtainable it was my job to pilfer it. I was not a bank robber, but I stole from stores, from yards, from pockets, from hands, from anything I thought I could get away with.

It wasn't a philosophy, it was more of a lifestyle. On a certain level my philosophy hasn't changed, I would still steal—if my family or I were starving, I would even kill to protect a loved one.

I was a thief, and I accepted that. That's what I was, and that's what everyone saw me as. Until one day.

A stranger caught me—red handed! I had never been caught so obviously before. I have been suspected many a time, but I'd always managed to hide or even drop the evidence. But this time there were no mistakes, I was caught.

I had just stolen a purse. Easy pickings really. I still don't know what went wrong. My escape route was clear, when out of nowhere a hand wrapped around my own, which was still holding the purse. With an almost gentle, yet unrelenting force he pushed me against a tree. And I, not being a violent man, offered no resistance.

He looked at me, I saw no sign of anger or disgust in his eyes. He looked at me not as a thief, but as a man.

"Why did you do this?" he simply asked.

Why? I had never been asked that before. "Because it was there," I thought, but, somehow, now that answer seemed almost insane and I could not get myself to say it aloud.

"What are you going to do to me?" I asked, looking around.

"It's up to you."

I didn't understand, was this a trick?

"We all choose how we want to be treated, how we see ourselves and how others see us."

"What do you see?" I found myself asking. I looked away, not able to face him or his response.

"I see..." he took his hand and placed it under my chin, lifting my head until our eyes met, "...a man at the crossroads."

From somewhere I felt something strange, I don't know if it was relief, or hope, or maybe even surrender.

His grip was no longer on me. I knew I could easily outrun him, yet I asked, "Am I free to go?"

He looked at me, perhaps he was squinting, "I don't know." He said, "Are you?"

"I won't do it again." The promise was halfhearted.

"There is only one here who you need to tell that to." He smiled.

I looked around, no one else was in sight. My heart was beating loudly, each beat seemed like an eternity. I didn't know what he meant at first.

He let me go. I left the purse with him. But I found something out about the strength of a heart, and not just any heart but *my heart*. A halfhearted promise made to one self has a hundred times the weight of a thousand angry strangers, or a thousand weeping victims.

The stranger may have been the first to see me as a man, and then I, shortly after, was the second, but soon there will be many. I guarantee it...to myself.

CHAPTER V

LOVE AND DEATH

At least

Being alone is not as bad as loneliness. For true loneliness is a state of mind that can surround and engulf, even when one is in a crowd. This was a desolate man who only wanted to feel connectedness. To belong. To be a part of. To not help another, but to share with another. Instead of understanding, to be understood. This was a man who truly knew that all men had the same fears and frailties. It was all a matter of trust, and letting the commonality surface. Belief, and acceptance...oh so many words that so few understood. How could he make them see?

Many learned, but at such a leisurely pace—it frustrated him. He wanted to teach, but there were so many unwilling to perceive the simplest realities. So many stubborn. So many that thought they were too good. Above everyone else. Too many. Too many. But what could he do about it?

He would think of something.

* * *

ELISE

Focus on beauty to take your mind off troubles. Zero in on

flawlessness to help wash away all the imperfection that surrounds. Amidst the pain and fear I can still find something to smile about. When all feels hopeless, and I know that I am lost, I have found a way out. I think of her.

My salvation.

Elise.

The consummate heavenly body. Her smile lights up my world. But she, like the sun, is unaware of her effect. I feel drawn towards her, and my head spins. I feel aglow when she's near, her gravitational effects make me want to stay by her side forever. Her laugh is so contagious it's almost embarrassing, one giggle from her and I want to laugh like a madman. I am definitely moonstruck.

Although thinking about her initially alleviates my worries and fears, eventually it just creates more anxiety. I fear, as would anyone in his or her right mind, perfection.

Do I fear not being good enough for her? Or do I fear really getting to know her, as there is only one way to come off a pedestal? Down. How could she possibly live up to expectations?

Elise—her name makes me tremble. Is it with fear or anticipation? She is a friend. An acquaintance. But I want more.

Liz wanted more. David wanted more. Is it safe for me to want more?

* * *

A CHILL IN THE NIGHT

The wind in the bar blew cold. She was like a breeze that blew him away. He felt the chill of her turn down. But like a leaf off a tree he silently drifted away.

"But not too far way," he thought, as he placed himself at a table far enough away from her so as to not be exposed to her bitter cold, yet close enough to watch her for the rest of the night.

He felt privileged to be able to witness her eloquence and grace. Her smile, from this distance, seemed to be genuine and warm, almost friendly. He sat watching grimly, yet comfortable, knowing that he was at a safe distance, protected from her coldness.

Watching. Witnessing the glacial display even though it was summer. Again and again.

Standing aloof, above all others, she, like a great sickle, sharp and deadly to each blade of grass that approached her. Little did she know that the first blade of grass she cut down tonight wasn't rotting in the soil shriveled and defenseless, but was watching her every move.

He noted, as the night wore on, that she drank very little. And she was still alone. Maybe she just came here to spread her coldness. Frigid or aloof? Frigidity could be slowly, carefully thawed, but if she was conceited there was nothing to be done. Arrogant to think that she could get away with it. Treating people like they were just meaningless toys to pass her time, to build up her ego. Did she count them all? Probably not, for numbers have some significance. She smiled at the trivialities that approached her, but she was probably laughing on the inside. Fools, all of them!

The first, biggest, fool of all sat back and observed, growing angrier with each pawn that was blown away by the queen. His temperature rose steadily, as she remained her same cold-blooded self.

He watched. He waited. He struggled with inner decisions bordering on turmoil. He fought to keep control. He needed to stay rational, to make clear-headed and well thought-out choices.

Maybe she was just waiting for the right one. Being choosy. It calmed him. "Please, God, let that be it!" he prayed. At this point he knew that if she was left alone, he couldn't let her stay in this world. He would see to it that she was alone, forever.

It was late. Not many others were in the street. She got into her car. Not many other cars were on the street. Only one that was of any importance to her. But she didn't notice anyone following. She was also nonchalant as she opened the door to her home. Easy access as a strong man pushed past her.

She swallowed her scream. "First mistake," he thought, as he knew that it was probably her only chance. Quickly he closed the door. Now no one would hear.

She tried to run, but he had a hold of her skirt. Then she spun around, arms flailing, and tried to land a well-placed kick. He dodged and made a grab for her hair. Grabbing hold of a small handful, it started to slip through his fingers, so he gave a violent tug, coming away with only a small handful of hair. This time she found her scream, and headed toward the other side of the room. He was much bigger than she, and faster...he was upon her before she took four steps. This time he got a good grip on her hair as it fell behind her, and with a tug that caused him to leave his feet, he brought her down, head to the ground, even though carpeted, there was a thud as head met floor. The only thing that could possibly be more sickening than that sound was the sound a second previous—the sound of a snapping neck.

He rolled the body over disgustingly, now he couldn't interview her. Damn bitch! She was as apathetic in death as she had been in life. Now he would have to leave unfulfilled. He had so many questions for her. He was no longer angry, just hurt.

Glancing around her home he let out a sigh. "Good thing she lives alone. I should have been more careful!"

Cleaning up the mess, and wiping away any evidence made him feel a little better; soon he would be his old jovial self.

* * *

NONCHALANT

"Hello Elise!"
"Steve, long time no see!"

"It's good to see you."

Her smile, at that point, melted my heart and from that point on my memory of our conversation is a bit blurry. I told her I hadn't been coming around much lately. We talked a little about Dave. For some reason our talk didn't flow as smooth as it usually did. At one point the gap in our conversation felt like I was falling into the Grand Canyon—the reason I didn't yell is because I knew she'd never hear me from on the other side. There was silence, but what turned my despair around was the fact that she wasn't antsy to go anywhere. We both stayed, baring the awkwardness. Maybe she wanted to be around me a fraction as much as I wanted to be around her. Believe me—a fraction was big! I smiled. She smiled.

I broke the silence by laughing.

"What's so funny?" She took a step back.

"I just..." was at a loss for words! I must have been beat red.

"You laughing at me?"

"No, No! I..." Why did I laugh? I didn't know! It was probably a nervous laugh. The only thing it should have possibly told her is that I am crazy! She shouldn't take offense. Maybe I just wanted her to laugh too.

She went on. "Because, if you are..." Oh, god, here it comes! "...then I'm going to tell your mother!" It was her turn to laugh.

It took me a moment or two to recover before I finally said, "Please don't! She won't let me play with you any more!"

"Play? What did you have in mind?"

"Tennis?"

"Singles?"

When I took a moment to answer she said, "Because I'm sick of doubles."

"Singles it is, then."

"It's a date!"

It is? My heart leapt! I had actually wanted to ask her out, and now it almost seems like I had done just that. Even though we had played tennis before, it was always doubles. Now singles did seem like a date.

Dr. Jack would be proud of me. With his encouragement I had come to this tennis club for the last three days with the sole purpose of seeking out Elise and asking her out. Finally, on the third day she showed up, and although I got cold feet—she warmed them up. Success!

* * *

KISMET

The odor of fear was in his nostrils, again. If it had been his fear he wouldn't have noticed it, but it was that of another young lady's. He felt the warmth of the blood on his hands cool, before he wiped it off. Another Prima Donna, another death.

This time it had been an alley as he could not wait to follow her all the way home. The anticipation raced through his blood vessels until his head felt like it would explode. He was following her on foot, saw a quick opportunity of a darkened alley, glancing around to see no other soul in sight he hurried forward, tackling her into the alley. He muffled her screams with blows to the face, eventually dragging her deep into the dark recesses where he put her out of her misery.

He didn't "interview" this one either. Again, no time. He began to vaguely realize that he was in it for the blood lust, and he really didn't want to know what made these women tick. He only knew he hated them and he wanted to cause their hearts to stop ticking.

In a panic he realized there was nowhere to wash up. He walked casually from the alley, blood on his hands, clothes and face. It was still warm on his body so he didn't wish to wash it off yet anyway. He would just have to be careful not to let anyone see him all the way home. Once he reached his car he figured he would be safe. He just needed luck on his side.

* * *

LOVE CUTS LIKE A KNIFE

"Steve, you've got blood on your hand."

Steve, taken aback at first, looked down at his hands. On his right hand there was a small cut on the knuckle of his thumb. "How'd I do that?" he questioned.

"Must be my wicked hits!" joked Elise, and they both forced a laugh. It was obvious that the tennis wasn't going well. It seemed that most time was spent chasing balls or saying, "excuse me," or "sorry."

They didn't play any real games, but each was hitting like they were in straight jackets. Steve wasn't hitting the ball hard enough to loosen up, and Elise aware of Steve's awkwardness, was probably trying to hit the ball too hard.

The cut, superficial and more of a smudge was a good excuse to quit playing. Each breathed a sigh of relief, then looked at each other with smiles.

"Too bad I got mutilated—I could have played all night," laughed Steve over a beer in the lounge.

"Do you want me to take you to the hospital?" Elise rolled her eyes and held back a laugh.

"Will they kiss it and make it all better?" Steve said with an exaggerated pout.

"Yes, and they'll change your diaper while you're there!"

"Hey, now you're getting personal!"

"Oh?" Elise looked into his eyes.

When he said nothing, in fact he was even fighting not to look away, she asked, "Is that something you're opposed to?"

"No!" Now he looked away. When he looked back, she was still watching him and his gaze met her beautiful eyes and he felt himself melting as he softly said, "I think I would like that."

She didn't say anything. She just sat there, smiling. He watched her looking at him. It was a little unnerving, but he liked it all the same. Why did she make him feel so shy? He never considered himself a shy person, but she made him feel flush, and his words, which normally flowed freely, had to be forced out his throat through numb lips.

He liked being around her, but he also realized that this wasn't going smooth. Maybe it wasn't meant to be. Everything felt so...magnified. The harder he tried to make this relationship work the more awkward it became. Their relationship had gone favorable until he had started thinking seriously about her. Maybe it was best to stay friends. She was the type of person that would be an excellent life-long friend. She was honest, sincere and...

Steve could only think about kissing her. Her lips. Her body. Her breasts, he envisioned touching them. He imagined pulling off her top just to look at them. He wanted to wrap his arms around her naked body. He wanted to pull her close and never let go. He wanted to make love to her...and...he wanted to love her.

But he knew they would always just be friends, and that made him sad, angry, and afraid all at the same time.

Sad that he might be losing something special.

Angry that the more he wanted it, it seemed to move farther away.

And afraid that he would never get another chance at a potential love like this.

So what's a man to do?

It was getting late and he told her so.

He walked her out to the parking lot. More silence. He had to break it! To say something!

"I would like to see you again."

"Am I invisible?" she asked.

"What...do you mean?"

"Aren't you seeing me now?" She did a little pirouette. She dazzled his eyes with her grace. "If you want to see me, then see me now." She opened her eyes as wide as they would go, and when he made no immediate response she added, "Unless you have something else to do."

"If I did, it's forgotten now." Steve smiled, as he finally regained his voice. Grabbing her hand, he headed to his car.

"Where are we going?" she asked as he opened the door for her.

"I know a great little park where we can have a picnic, but first we need to get food and drink.

Shifting gears, Steve revved up the car and pulled away. "Shifting gears," thought Steve, "nice little trick, without which we'd be forever afraid, and stuck."

* * *

FEELING WHOLE

Sitting in limbo. Afraid to continue, yet anxious about the possibility of stopping. An empty hole inside that only the blood of others could fill. Yet, with the weight of each victim the hole became larger, until the victims, the killing, were all he could think about. It consumed him just as he consumed the people. It was all their fault. He knew it was really he who was the victim. He could either consume them, or stop and let the emptiness consume him. There was nothing he feared more than the emptiness.

* * *

TO FALL

In love. Maybe not love at first sight, but more like love at first thought. There was a small, secret part of him that knew long before he could ever say to anyone, including to himself, and especially to her, that he was in love. Love he had never felt before. Not like this.

Maybe puppy love in the past; in college, in high school, in his dreams. But never like this.

Did she return the love? He, at times, tried desperately to read the signs, but at a certain level, it didn't really matter. His intense feelings were enough, maybe all he could handle, at least for the time being. He knew there would come a time when he would long to have his love returned in full, and maybe that was the time he would tell her of his love. But as for now it was enough, more than enough, as he rode a high that he had never known before.

"One step at a time," he thought, as he took her hand and crossed the street.

* * *

FELLED

Terrified. Panic.

Her heart is racing, as is his.

A knife opens a wound. Her blood sprays him like that of a fire hose. Blood seems endless until the continued slashing causes flesh to tear and the panic to turn to disbelief. The blood, still so very warm, no longer spurts, but flows.

Slowly, as the thought of death sets in, the blood is now seeping, as a steady stream, but like molasses, sticky, and soon the eyes glaze over. The once racing pulse is now faint and irregular. The blood looks darker, as it is no longer alive, and it coagulates in pools around the body. The stopping of the heart is more of an acceptance than an event—a relief for both the victim and the killer.

* * *

MURDERS?

The daily newspaper started being delivered to me. I didn't subscribe. One day it just started showing up on my doorstep. I paid the bill when it came, even though I seldom read it. Maybe I would glance through it once in a while. But it never became a routine in my day. Usually I brought it to work and would leave it in the break room. By the end of the day it would be picked through and scattered about to where I knew it was being well utilized.

On one Saturday, in which I had an appointment to see Dr. Jack, I just grabbed the paper on my way out and threw it on my passenger seat because I was in too much of a hurry to take it back inside. The headlines glared up at me—"Murder! Again!"—for the whole twenty minute ride.

I didn't read any more than those glaring headlines, but I was having trouble getting them out of my head even once the session with the doctor began.

I talked. He listened. I said nothing of importance, and he made few comments. Things were going pretty well with me. I was happy. Maybe "numb" was a better word, but at least I was in no immediate pain. The session was shaping up to be one of the most uneventful ones we had ever had.

Then, something strange happened. He brought up the murder, or murders—as I found out from him that there had been a series of murders. It looked like a serial killer was on the loose.

We talked of death. Death in general was fine. It denoted the passing of time. It was a natural process; everything died so that there could be new growth. Yet, death in specific always seemed to have a tragic feel to it. Someone always died of something in particular, be it a disease, and accident, or whatever. A specific death never felt normal to those close. Death wasn't a part of a process, only an end. Only when one steps back from the intimacy of a particular death to take a grand view could death be seen as something acceptable and natural. In the case of these murders, obviously there was a killer, but did every death have a killer? A suicide's killer was himself. How about an accident or an old age death? Who was the killer then?

God?

I felt very strange during and after our talk. I couldn't place my finger on the reason for my peculiar feeling. Certainly our talk toward the end had been on the strange side, but it really wasn't that uncommon. Our conversations over the last year had been anything but what I would expect to be the normal conversations between a patient and psychiatrist. Dr. Jack was an interesting person, not your normal boring psychiatrist, but that is precisely why I continued to see him, and why I considered him such a help.

But today was different. Somehow. Someway. Today was different.

It felt as if I was being shamed. Certainly the good doctor didn't think that I...I shuddered at the thought. I must be reading him wrong. Certainly there was no way that he could think I was responsible in any way. I vowed to purge these thoughts from my mind, for how else could I continue to see him if I thought he had any doubts about me.

I wanted to forget. I needed to forget. I would forget.

* * *

ANOTHER

She started to remove her clothes.

"What are you doing?"

She stopped unbuttoning her blouse. Her small, firm breasts were barely visible between the fold of her shirt. He saw how small her trembling hands were as they lingered around her stomach. She shot him a quick glance and then looked to her feet. For the first time he really looked at her, noticing how small and childlike in appearance she was. She was tiny.

"Please don't hurt me," she whispered in a minute voice that was even more small than she.

It seemed that she was willing to give herself up to him, because she didn't want to get hurt, and she knew she was no match for him physically. She didn't know that he wasn't here to rape her. He had a more permanent solution in mind.

He gazed down upon her elfin frame as he stepped forward. Taking her would be like taking his own daughter. Nausea grew in his stomach, and hands went from his fist clenched in rage to clenched around her neck. With only a few breaths left she grabbed at him. What was she doing? He monetarily loosened his hold as he looked to her hand reaching between his legs. This was one sex-crazed chick! But the thought made him angry and he tightened his grasp around her neck. With one last effort she had her hand in his pants and with fingernails she dug into soft flesh there, which was painful but not lethal. She looked at him with startled eyes as she crumbled, dying to the floor.

He looked at her, as she lay lifeless on the floor, almost with admiration. One of her breasts was now exposed as her blouse had swung to one side. He gently covered it and rolled her over to a more comfortable position. When he went to clean up, he made sure he cleaned her up first. Taking extra care to clean her hands and fingernails so as to leave no evidence of him behind.

As he turned to go, he looked back at what he knew was no sex-crazed child, but someone who was a survivor, who would do anything to live. For he had seen the surprise in her eyes that she had found him limp and not turned on. She had misjudged him—he was not a rapist! If she had been right, if he had been hard at the time her fingernails had found his penis, he knew it could have been him lying on the floor back there instead of her.

* * *

THE DOCTOR IS IN

I had another of my reoccurring dreams about falling. I don't remember anything else about the dream. But on this morning it happened to be one in which I was scheduled to see Dr. Jack. Nonetheless the subject never came up.

"You and Elise?" Dr. Jack wanted to know about the budding relationship. He had been there from the start. He had been the one to encourage my movement forward. He had unearthed from me an inner will. A desire. He must have sensed my spirit for a girl who was just a name to him; he must have heard the longing in my voice when I said her name. Without his subtle pushes toward her, I'm not sure I would have gotten to know her grace. Would I have had the courage? Maybe, eventually. But maybe it would have been too late. I was aware of how much I owed to the good doctor.

"It's great! I can't believe how great a relationship can be." I did not withhold my exuberance.

"First time?"

"Huh?"

"In love."

"I've never known a love like this, but 'in love'...I...I guess that I am."

"That's great!"

"I haven't told her yet. This is really the first time I've told myself. I don't want to complicate things." I was talking fast.

"No need to tell her."

"Really?"

"Why, do you feel the need?"

"No! I just thought...was afraid, that you would encourage me to tell her."

"I don't see any burning desire from you to tell her. Enjoy where you're at."

"Yes," I readily agreed.

"Telling someone you're in love is a personal matter. You should never feel forced into it. Some couples say it all the time, some—never. The feeling is more important than the words. Leave it to man to take a concept as complex as love—as well as the most wondrous feeling in the universe, and reduce it down to three *important* words."

"So many in this world crave love, and can never find it, that it is almost a crime to deny these feelings. To stand aloof from love may be the most iniquitous sin."

"Just live with the passion you feel. Let the love you feel bring out the you you always wanted to be. Let the real you come out. It's always safe in love. Love protects us. If love goes then retreat if you have to, but while love is here take advantage and enjoy!"

* * *

SOME THINGS ARE TOO BIG FOR WORDS

Sometimes they don't have to say "no." Sometimes it exudes from their pores. The arrogance. It is not always shown, nor covered, by mere words. Sometimes it's the way they talk and not what they say. It can be gay, it can be straight, but it is always rotten, and hopeless. Useless. It serves no purpose but to alienate or belittle. Whether it's black, white, or shades of gray there is an evilness about it that stands out and masks all the other characteristics, but only to those who can truly see.

Isn't it ironic that those that think they are better are the worse? Rich, poor—it usually didn't matter. There were so many spoiled apples, he sometimes wondered if it wouldn't be easier to just chop down the whole tree.

Let God start again.

* * *

MORE BIG WORDS IN A SPOT OF TROUBLE

I reached out to touch her. She pulled away. Slowly, almost unnoticeably, yet I could sense the recoil.

I walked to the other end of the room. I stared back at her, but before she could return my gaze, I looked away.

The tension. You could cut it with a knife, like the one that cut out my heart. I was angry. I was afraid. I was confused. She was...stubborn.

We had had our first fight. None so bitter was than the first fight from a couple whom had fooled themselves into thinking themselves incapable. Angry thoughts, angry words. Love doesn't leave room.

But now I was pissed! It was all over, I was sure. She was sure. There was nothing more to say.

Angry words can never be taken back. Shouts—even worse— they would echo in the heavens forever and make it so obvious that these two should not be together.

He hated her. Like he had never hated before!

Elise had fallen. His eyes would never see her the same.

The argument was over nothing, but that was trivial because it showed him the real person he was dealing with. Stubborn! Stubborn, just plain and simple. Good thing he found out now before he got too close.

He cursed her under his breath.

She shot her evil eyes his way.

He wanted to leave.

Walk away and not look back.

He wanted to, but couldn't. He stayed there. With her. In agony. No one spoke for years, decades—until a tiny voice came from nowhere.

He had to lean forward to hear. He didn't want to listen to anything this foul creature had to say but, nonetheless, he found himself involuntarily leaning forward.

In his imagination he heard the words "I love you." He stepped back, knowing now that he would never say these words, that had been echoing in his brain for the last few days, to her.

He tried to quiet his infernal brain to hear what she was about to say, but her lips were already moving. They were in phase with the ones in his brain. He read her lips, but it was there in her eyes too, "I love you. I don't want to fight with you."

"I love you too!" his brain screamed. Aware his lips weren't moving, Steve rushed forward and embraced her. Lifting her up and off her feet, he spun her around. With his face pressed to her neck, the smell of her hair in his nostrils, he whispered the words that had been in his brain, but that came from his heart, "I love you."

* * *

ANOTHER TOUGH SPOT

A bloodstain on his wrist the next morning soiled the rest of his day. It was a missed drop of blood from the girl of the night before. A piece of death still lingered with him the next day. A reminder of the chaos from the previous night broke the tranquillity of the next day.

His mind was in a cloud. He tried to surmise what he was feeling, and couldn't. Guilt? He was sure that the ones who were left, the ones he hadn't gotten to, and possibly never would, should feel much more guilty than he. Remorse? Yes, he did feel a bit sorry for himself.

But by the end of the day he had figured out that the thing that bothered him most about the small bloodstain left on his wrist from the night before was that it showed that he was getting careless. His meticulous scrubbing up somehow wasn't as meticulous as it once was. And how about the crime scene, had he been as careless cleaning that up?

Was he one of those waiting, hoping to be caught? Was his subconscience leaving subtle clues behind for the police to find? Would his mistakes get more frequent and obvious? He had seen it happen before, but those others were criminals: his killing was serving a purpose. He was performing a public service; those others had been just crazy.

He vowed to be more careful in the future, because if he got caught, there would be no one to carry on his work.

He brought his wrist up to his mouth and sucked at the bloodstain until it was gone. Noting the salt taste in his mouth, he wondered if it was from the blood or from his own sweat.

* * *

STEPS

"I love you!"

She smiled back at Steve. "I love you, too."

Now that the cat was out of the bag, neither could say it, nor hear it, enough. Things were perfect, Steve was happy, Elise was happy. The next step was obvious; it was time to express that love in ways besides words.

Steve thought about making love to her often, but he didn't want to push it. He wanted it to be natural. Just as verbalizing their love had happened, he wanted their physical expression to be as spontaneous. He knew that when the time was right, it would happen, and just like every thing else with Elise—it would be perfect.

* * *

WOULD YOU MIND?

From deep within him, the anger would rise. Like having a faucet on a geyser, he knew how to turn the switch, sending his rage bursting forth upon a defenseless victim. Defenseless, but deserving.

It was his choice to turn it on, but once on it was like he would turn senseless during these moments of shear rage. Deaf, dumb, and blindly his rage would control him. He felt like a puppet to the inner volcano released. It was totally reactionary. Like a predator devouring his prey. He could step back and coldly observe his actions as if he was watching a movie. He was the director and he made decisions without feeling a part of them. This director demanded cleanliness and order. He controlled the final results without controlling the particular actions. He left the individual actions to instinct, as his thought process was too slow to hunt and kill. He took care of the aesthetics.

One girl in particular he didn't need much instinct for. She seemed to cooperate. Maybe she thought he would go easy on her. She simply froze. Waiting for the end. Maybe that was her strategy. They say to do that with bears; play dead and most often they will leave you alone. Once the threat of you is minimized they lose interest. Their instincts to defend and kill are greatly reduced.

But this was not a bear. It was a human predator. And his rage was still there, and as his instincts diminished his mind could no longer be a distant observer. His mind tried to rationalize her behavior, as she lay prone before him, waiting patiently for the kill or his mercy. She was totally vulnerable to him. Was she trying to make him feel guilty? But he knew she was not defenseless, not as defenseless as those she stood above and judged. Turning down one lonely man after another as if to say that no man was good enough for her. She flaunted her imagined superiority with every turndown. How could someone like that be vulnerable in any way? No, she was merely pretending to be something she was not. It was a trick.

Did she think him a fool?

His rage boiled until it turned to something else, something he had not felt before. His head spun, his throat grew dry.

Still she lay there, a wolf in sheep's clothing.

He could not swallow.

He stepped forward; and yet she made no movement. Her hands were calmly at her side. Sure the look of terror was on her face, but that had to be faked—for he knew that she still thought herself better than him.

With more violence than he intended he tore away her disguise. Nevertheless, she offered no resistance; she lay before him as if frozen. He tossed her clothes to the side. She was now naked, but for her panties and bra.

Her eyes were wide but she continued her ice cube front.

Was she dead already? Heart attack? In a panic, he placed his hand on her chest. He felt her heart beating as if it was attempting to leave her chest. She was still very much alive!

He noticed blood on her stomach from when he ripped off her clothes. "You didn't even say "Ow," he thought as he touched the blood and smeared it with his fingertips. Her stomach muscles contracted and her arms tensed up, but still he could see she was fighting to stay motionless.

"Damn bitch still trying to fool me!" Did he say it out loud or was it just that strong in his own thoughts that it rang in his ears?

"I'm not a threat, huh?" This time it was his thoughts, but it repeated over and over in his head as he removed his clothes, carefully folding them in a neat pile in the corner of the room.

"Still you don't move!" he said to her as he came upon her.

He climbed aggressively on top of her. Her arms pulled up as if trying to meekly ward him off.

"It's too late now!" he screamed into her face, pinning her arms to her side.

He tried to enter her, but she was tight and his penis slipped past her entry point.

"A girl like you can't get turned on!" he screamed, and this time, with the force of a punch he came down upon her again. She winced, as he was successful this time.

Each thrust was like a blow, and when he thought that it wasn't causing enough pain he included a fist to the face. It wasn't long before her face was a bloody mess and her lower body was a sticky mess.

She was in convulsions as he climbed off her. She was choking on her own vomit.

"Hold that dirty stuff down, you bitch!" he said as he choked her until he was sure that no more vomit would come up.

"There!" he said as he triumphantly walked away from the lifeless body. He knew that this night his victory was minimal, however, as he had much clean up work to do.

"It's not worth it," he muttered to himself as he set about his chores.

With a sigh he said, "Damned are the chosen ones."

* * *

AND THE TIME IS

Two lovebirds sat alone in a park, they touched often, but spoke little until the girl broke the silence by saying, "You love me."

"Oh yeah?" He laughed. "How do you know?"

"Because I know you're not a liar."

"Can you tell other than by my words?"

"Yes. I can feel your love. It permeates me. I breathe in the breath that you exhale and it sends molecules of love into my system where they corrupt my being."

"Corrupt?" Steve smiles.

"Perhaps corrupt is not strong enough a word..." Elise's smile grew.

"Not strong enough!"

"No. Your love obliterates me. It not only surrounds me, but engulfs me. Your love has taken over my soul. Your love is all."

"I..." Steve thought for a moment, then swallowed and said, "I want to give all of me to all of you."

Elise just watched him, nodding slightly.

"And I want all of you."

Her smile grew, and she blushed slightly.

"What I'm trying to say..."

"Yes, yes?" She suppressed a laugh.

"I want to make love to you."

"Here?"

"No!" Now it was his turn to be embarrassed. "I think it would be best if we found a more private place." Steve laughed.

"Like behind that tree?" She giggled.

"Naw, the squirrels would be watching!"

"How about in the lake."

"Oh! Wouldn't the fish be trilled!"

"How about the top of a mountain?"

"Since none are within view, how about my place?"

"I want to," she turned serious, "but can you give me just a little more time? Please?"

For a second he felted rejected, but quickly recovered and said, "Take your time, I would wait forever for you. I don't plan on going anywhere."

Elise rolled over, and threw herself into his arms and gave him the most substantial hug he had ever had. He kissed her, and they rolled in their embrace to the edge of their blanket. His hands wandered and her hands found, and for a moment he thought that maybe she had been serious to do it right in the park.

Steve waited. He had always considered himself a patient man, but he couldn't help bringing up the sex topic a few more times. She said that he would be the first to know when she was ready. It frustrated him because he knew that it would be wonderful.

He was seeing Dr. Jack much less often these days. Immediately after David's coming out surprise he had increased his visits with Dr. Jack to twice a week, but now his visits were down to once every other month. Dr. Jack had been the first to know about Steve's feelings for Elise and was also the first he told of his sexual frustration too. Perhaps Elise knew it, could feel it, but Steve never said a word to her about his anxiety.

"Can you tell her how you feel?" Dr. Jack inquired.

"About everything, but this."

"Is this really that big of a deal?"

"Maybe not."

"Perhaps you caught her at a bad time of the month."

"This has been going on for more than a month."

Dr. Jack made a noncommittal reply of, "Oh," but he sat up in his chair just a little. "Perhaps she wants to wait until she's married."

"We never even talked about marriage. She said she would make love, but she seems to be just making me wait."

"Maybe she is afraid."

"Believe me, Doc, this girl is afraid of nothing. She's as much the aggressor as I. I can't help thinking that she is just teasing me."

"Is she the type?"

"I don't know...I don't know anything any more. I am so confused."

"Maybe she's not the one for you?" It was more a question than a statement.

Dr. Jack had a way of cutting through the crap. "God, I love her so! If she is not the one for me then there is none!" Steve was almost in tears.

"At this point, then, you must decide, does she bring you more pleasure or pain?"

"I think I would die without her!"

"Then what is the real question here?"

"I just...want to know what I can do..."

"Perhaps there is nothing you can do."

Steve fought back tears as his body was starting to shake, and with pleading, red eyes he looked to Dr. Jack for an answer, a sign, or comfort.

Dr. Jack came forward, placing an arm around Steve. Dr. Jack had seen before where a strong and confident man becomes a blithering wimp all for the love of a woman. He knew it wasn't the love that was the venomous part, but the games that were. Deadly games of the heart where the female of the species definitely had the upper hand. "Tell me about it," he said in a tranquil voice.

Steve tried to hide his face in his hands, but Dr. Jack pushed on. "What are you feeling?"

"Alone." And the sobs came.

Dr. Jack lifted Steve's head up with a gentle, but strong hand and asked, "So what do you want from Elise?"

"I love her so much. I love her so much!" Steve said over and over.

"Do you think that maybe she doesn't know it?"

"Yes! I'm sure that she does." Steve was silent for a few minutes and Dr. Jack did nothing to push. Finally Steve said, "And at one time it didn't matter. It didn't matter at all." Steve knew he was being silly, petty, but he could not get his emotions to subside to his embarrassment. He pushed on. "But now it's different. Things have changed. Now I care. It does matter."

"What matters?" probed the doctor.

"I need to know, that she loves me as much as I love her!" Then the heavy tears came, and Dr, Jack did nothing to quiet them. After a moment's hesitation he hugged Jack's face to his chest. How a woman could mess up a man, yes, Dr. Jack had seen it before, many a time.

Dr. Jack remained professional, quickly wiping a tear from his own eye.

* * *

DEATH TAKES A DAY OFF

To watch falling leaves float gently to the ground is a peaceful way to pass an autumn day. The once plain green leaves, now multiple colors sail ceremoniously to the ground. We think of them as a serene way to show the passing of time, the changing of seasons. A gentle breeze takes them away on their last journey. They go willingly, doing their fancy individualized pirouettes as they exit.

If only we could hear their screams.

A man, who had been watching the leaves, knowing that there is enough death on this day, goes home alone.

* * *

IF I AWAKE

Isolation.

I wish I could express pain. I wish fear could flow from me into my pen, so by putting that dread to paper I could then crumple it up and toss it away.

I wish to sweat out frustration through my pores and my disillusionment could run down my cheeks as tears.

Let me release all my troubles in my dreams. Let me merely understand my questions, for I fear not being able to tolerate the knowledge of the answers.

I walk, but I fear running.

A single star in the nighttime sky shines but for me. I have never felt so alone; I have never been so crowded with thought.

I walk a straight line, but my thoughts move in circles.

A whisper on a clear, crisp night stops at a single ear. Rumors spread; Exaggerations grow, but truth is like an explosion. The explosion separates us, as was designed from the start. The illusion of closeness is burned in the flames. The truth separates us. For the truth is that we are separate. Love is but ashes in the wind. All else but solitude is a dream.

Nothing matters. Matter is nothing.

Reality is an island. Seclusion is peace. All else is chaos.

Distant memories—tomorrow forgotten. Dreaming of tomorrow, but longing for today.

Alone. Again. But this has always been the truth. All else had been a mirage.

* * *

It was all a dream.

Only a dream. He wasn't sure of his reaction to this realization. Was he feeling happiness, or resignation, or...nothing?

Steve awoke alone. God, of course there was no one who loved him—not on this earth anyway, or in this lifetime. There was no love for him, and no one to love. Steve had always been alone. It was solely in his dreams that he could ever have a hope of love. With eyes wide, all fairy dust blew away—it must be the wind from his eyelashes as he opened his eyes. The mind's eye is so much more luminous than the vision from the retina. Even the most beautiful painting, when scrutinized too closely, becomes nothing but brush strokes.

Alone.

His latest dream...what had been her name? He blocked it out. He blocked out her name, her face, her touch, her smile, and his feelings for her—just as he blocked out the ringing phone.

Alone.

His fantasies sometimes seemed so real that he thought he could reach out and touch them. His fantasies were a fun pastime, but he tried not to take them too seriously. He must remain himself, and not lose himself in one of them. They were only real if he let her be. He blocked out the face he loved, but the ringing of the phone, once again, broke his concentration.

The damn phone. For day after day the phone seemed to ring continuously. Until by the fourth day he could stand it no more. He picked it up.

"Hello." His voice was meek, even his ears didn't recognize it.

"Steve?" A vaguely familiar voice, weakening his defenses.

"Yes."

"Where have you been?"

"Elise." There was a pause, he fought to stay silent, he fought to keep a smile from his face, and the biggest fight was with his heart. It was a three second fight. "Sorry, I've been out."

"Man, I didn't know what happened, I thought you'd moved...or died." Her voice cracked.

Steve closed his eyes, knowing some dreams were too real to ignore.

Tears were streaming down his face as he said, "I missed you."

Then all was quiet. The phone line might as well have been dead but for an occasional whispered "I love you," by one or the other.

The sharing of space, the sharing of a mind-set, the sharing of a dream. Maybe that is all that it took to make a dream real—the shared belief in it.

When one has a dream, he or she is crazy. And two sharing the same dream may also be crazy, but at least each has someone to turn to, and shared insanity is almost spiritual. It's all about belief. Beliefs make you crazy. And beliefs set you free. It has been said that the only true free men are in asylums.

Whether it's belief in a voiceless, faceless God, or a belief in another of the frail, vulnerable, confused, unreliable, members of the human species, beliefs are the stuff that dreams are made of.

Steve opened his eyes, and in a clear, strong voice said, "I need you."

The fact that there was no response, but for the muffle sobs on the other end, didn't detour Steve, he was resolute as he asked, "Can

I come over."

He was sure that he heard a "yes" come across the phone lines, but even if he was deceiving himself—he didn't care—he was going over there anyway. And with one more "I love you," he hung up the phone and got ready to substantiate his dream.

* * *

IF SHE WAKES

The blood still flowed, and that meant that she still lived. How could this be so? It seemed there was enough blood for ten men. True, she was a large woman—what a fight she had put up!

He was so tired. He just wanted to go home. He was tempted to go home, leaving her half-alive. She would continue to bleed, maybe to death, but she would still be triumphant. Such will to live, when she so obviously deserved to die, spat in the face of God. Her angel of mercy was here, to relieve her of her life, but it was he who was growing weary as she refused to die. So damn ignorant was the one who refused to accept the inevitable.

He stepped back from the situation. She was fighting with unconsciousness. He was struggling with his lack of desire to finish his job. More than being tired, for he was breathing hard, he was weary. Weary from all the deaths. Did they really serve a purpose? Was he really having an effect? There were so many. Too many for one man. Too many physically, to say nothing of the mental anguish. He was drained. There was something else he wanted from that half alive woman, but he refused to think about it. His denial was most tiring of all.

He walked into the next room. Sitting in a chair, he found the remote control and turned on the TV. He would pass the time away, waiting for her to die. Waiting to regain his strength. Waiting, always waiting. So much idle time and so little action. TV was a nice escape.

After flicking the remote in rapid fashion he finally settled on a show. He watched for about a half an hour, then suddenly clicked it off, deciding there was too much violence on TV.

He got up to check on his latest "work." He approached the next room with caution, although he anticipated finding her dead. To his astonishment she was gone!

Panic gripped him. He swung toward the front door, almost expecting the police to come rushing in. He started to shake. How had he been so careless? How could she get away, she was so close to death? He fought to regain that numb feeling that gave him the success at killing. But the more he fought, the more the fears inside grew. The more his mind raced, thinking up endless scenarios, all of which led to a bad ending for him, the more he realized that each second could be vital. To run, go find her, or to stay and piss his pants—his decisions detonated in his brain. His body was feeling every possible feeling—all at once, while his brain was numb. His brain was incapable of making a decision.

He was shivering. But a warmth soon came. It was contained in one area, but slowly spreading—between his legs. For he relived himself, it wasn't a purposeful thing but perhaps it was a subconscious gift, as it took him out of his stupor and allowed him to hear for the first time a noise. More of a groan than a noise, he realized only now that it had been almost continuous. It was coming from the next room over, the kitchen.

He turned from the door to the kitchen, and he saw her, lying in a crumpled ruin in the corner of the kitchen.

A guttural moan was coming from the bloodied figure. She was still holding on to her precious life.

He took a few deep breaths, trying to calm himself, as he watched her futile attempts to crawl across the floor. It was pitiful. Why didn't she just accept death? Someone who cared about life so much shouldn't have been so stuck-up when she knew life to the fullest. Now she was grasping at straws.

He wondered, if he did let her live, would she change her ways? Was this lesson enough to make someone change his or her ways? It would make quite an interesting experiment.

He approached her slowly, almost gently. But just as deftly his hand reached up to a pot on the stove and when he reached striking distance he brought the pan down with a fury upon her head.

It was a definite overkill, but with this one he had to be sure.

He felt a little remorse at having to abandon a potential experiment, but letting her survive would be a definite threat to his freedom, and God knows, he couldn't carry out his mission from a jail cell.

Yes, this mission had caused him to make many a sacrifice.

* * *

SLEEPING...AGAIN

She opened the door before he knocked. He kissed her before she spoke. Their cautious eyes searched each other for an anger that wasn't there. Each one's smiles answered the others biggest questions.

It was like two lost souls reincarnated from a hundred lifetimes ago to once again find their soul mate. They stood at the door, embraced for what seemed between seconds and timelessness, which the clock would have told as thirty minutes.

It was the dinosaur syndrome; each had felt like extinction was around the corner, then to suddenly find another like themselves was too good to be true. Another of the same species. Someone who knew. Who understood. Someone to love.

But it was true.

Tears streamed down the face of Steve. Most were his own. Tears of joy, but mostly tears of relief.

"I love you." Steve knew he would never let her get away. He knew that all would work out, as long as there was love, nothing could send them too far off the path. But the length or direction of the path really didn't matter as long as it was wide enough for two.

"I love you, too," Elise answered. All her fears seemed to blow away with his breath. More than hear, she could feel his love. Just being with him, near him, was all that mattered. He calmed her soul. She felt like he was a part of herself, a good part, strong, safe. But yet, it wasn't him...she realized that it was actually her! These were the parts of her that she liked, he just brought them out. Steve made it safe, made it advantageous, to come out. She loved him, but more importantly she loved these things that were a part of her, parts of her she had denied. They came out because of him, but they had been there all along in her. All along she had been the person that stood in front of him at this present moment. Now it didn't seem so impossible that a man like Steve could love someone like her. She felt warm inside, and powerful.

Steve saw the love in her eyes, but did he see something more? He sensed something in her that had not been there before. Was it desire? He dared not go there. He went away. Physically, by turning; and mentally, by taking his thoughts far away. But it was still there. Weighing heavy in the room. He denied it, but he couldn't stop from feeling it. His desire for her was strong. But now was it returned?

She pulled him back to her, not with a look or a word but with a tug. "C'mere, you."

Interlocking her hand in his she led him away. Neither said a word, but he could hear her breathing and his heart thundered in his ears.

* * *

IT MUST BE IN THE AIR

Death. One after another. Seemingly all the same. But something changed. It had been the silent one. Always beware of the silent ones. She had said nothing. Done nothing. She just lay there in silence. Waiting. Waiting for what?

It angered him. It frustrated him. It had turned him on.

A rapist. No! Not he!

But since that damned silent girl it was all different now. She had forever changed him and his mission.

He had hated the killing. The blood. But somebody had to do it. He would fulfill his mission even as he dreaded it. He loathed the violence, and was turned off by death.

...Until that night.

...And since.

He has left every death since that fateful day with an erection.

But he was not an animal! Why would God curse him so?

He could not help it! As vigorously as he tried to fight the feeling it only grew until he feared it would consume him. He feared becoming an animal and losing his clear and rational thought process. He feared losing his humanity.

He now got hard just thinking about the deaths. What was he becoming?

What was he to do?

* * *

GOODNIGHT...NOT GREAT

Her touch. Her look. Her bedroom.

Her desire.

Steve's head spun.

Their hands were still interlocked, but with her free hand she attempted to unbuckle his belt.

She kissed him.

Both were breathing heavily.

He brought their interlocked hands up and pressed the back of her hand to his cheek. He felt the desire rise within him. Had he ever wanted anything as much as he wanted her right at that moment?

She pressed her body against his, and he knew his desire was shared. Passion wafted up between them and around them. He knew their hearts were more entwined than their fingers or lips could ever be.

Something inside of him fought against his desire. To protect him from being hurt. To shield him from unrequited desire. The little boy in him wanted to run. But all thoughts of fear were extinguished when he looked into her eyes.

The glory of her eyes. Beautiful. Shining. The eyes of a lighthouse to a lost sailor. Lead the way. Lead the way. Trust in the light of her eyes. He wanted to be swept away in her waves of passion. He was willing to risk losing a part of himself, to gain the universe.

Together they walked, as if dancing, over to the bed. She tumbled down, pulling him with her.

He laughed, but suddenly she grew serious. Taking his face in her hands, she made sure their eyes made contact when she spoke, "I love you. But I'm afraid..."

He waited, but when she said nothing more he spoke. "There is nothing to fear. I love you."

"I know." Her smile melted his heart. "And I want to make love with you, but...things haven't always worked out."

"I love you, not sex...I can't imagine it being anything less than wondrous, but if it doesn't live up to our expectations I will still love you. I will always love you. I just want to be with you. To express myself to you."

"And I want you. Honest!"

"I know that." Steve smiled and shrugged his shoulders.

"I have been...close...before, and I never make it. I get hysterical, I don't know why I just can't seem to make it through, the feelings overwhelm me and I run, I just don't know why I..." Elise was talking so fast Steve couldn't understand her.

Placing a hand to her lips he got her to stop, then he said, "We don't have to do anything you're not ready for."

"But I want to. Really I do!" Getting playful, she bounced on the bed next to him and into his arms.

"I'm not sure what you're trying to tell me then."

"I just want to make you aware. I don't want to lose you. In the past...I panic, and guys leave. I couldn't bear losing you. I want you to understand if I get afraid. Maybe that's impossible—for I don't even understand it myself. But even if you don't understand it, love me enough to stay. I can't lose you!"

"I'm not going anywhere. Just relax." He was rubbing her back.

Clothes came off. Two naked bodies clung to each other.

They rolled from one end of the bed to the other, flesh against flesh, kissing, stroking, and grabbing. When Steve could hold off no longer he smoothly persuaded her onto her back. Then with hands still caressing her breast, neck, and face, he straddled her and found the moist spot between her legs.

He entered her without a problem.

He sensed her tense up. He tried to be more gentle.

Her body went from being warm and soft to cold and clammy.

Her eyes were closed. Steve stroked one of her breasts, and it was obvious that she was holding her breath.

Suddenly her eyes flew wide, "Get off me! Get off me! GET OFF!" she screamed.

Steve saw the anger in her eyes, he knew she wanted to yell more, but she bite her lip and glared at him.

Finally she simply said, "Go."

Steve moved to the edge of the bed, confused. His head was spinning and his breathing was still heavy. He put one foot to the floor...

Was this the girl he loved? Panic rose within him. He evened his breathing until he felt more calm. Him freaking out wouldn't help the situation. He looked over at Elise. She was shaking. She wasn't even aware that he was still there. He wanted to sneak out and come back to the real Elise. One question haunted him and he couldn't leave until he had an answer. "Was this the girl he loved?"

He was suddenly very cold sitting on the edge of the bed, as he became aware of his nakedness.

She wanted him to leave.

His instincts said to leave.

His shivering body told him to find his clothes and exit.

Elise was no longer aware he was there, she wouldn't notice his exit.

How could he be a man and let the woman he loved scream at him at such a vulnerable time?

So why was he still here? He placed his other foot gently to the floor.

But the question, the unanswered question, still haunted him.

He glanced back at Elise. She was naked and uncovered, curled up in a ball. Eyes closed, she was shivering—she must be cold too. Steve looked at their clothes scattered on the floor.

Elise was bare.

Which girl did he fall in love with?

The pretend Elise—who was perfect? Who would be everything to him? Who dressed right, and kissed right, said all the right things, and who acted perfect? The one he would never fight with? The one who would understand his flaws...?

Or the Elise that lay shivering, vulnerable on the bed, who needed someone to understand her flaws?

So was this the girl he loved?

He reached over and put a hand on her shoulder. She pulled away and rolled over, away from him, keeping her eyes still shut tight.

He climbed back into bed. Being careful not to touch her, he got as close to her as he dared. He then reached down and pulled a blanket up over both of them. He listened to her breathing steady as her shivering stopped.

Her breath finally grew even and deep as they lay there, together, yet separate. He felt her warmth, as his eyes grew heavy.

He started to doze when he felt her toes touch his knee. He opened his eyes in time to see her turn towards him. Her eyes were still closed as she embraced him, grabbing onto him. He opened his arms and took her in. The two bodies melded into one, sharing the warmth, clinging. They fell asleep that way.

Steve woke about an hour later, Elise still in his arms. He slowly opened his eyes to see her looking at him. She was smiling and that made him smile until they both laughed.

He kissed her on the forehead. She snuggled her head into his chest.

"I could have you hold me forever," she said in a shy voice.

They lay that way, smiling.

"I have never felt so relaxed," she stated contently.

"I love you," he breathed.

Together, with peaceful thoughts, they stay, serene and in love.

Time passed, as their breath was synchronous.

He sensed her tiny sudden movement. It's as if her heart skipped a beat.

"Oh my God!" she said.

"What's the matter?"

"I think I should be alone."

"Huh?"

"I think you should leave."

"What's wrong?"

"Oh my God."

Now Steve started to become concerned. He put his arm around her.

She pulled away. "I don't think you should do that."

"Elise. You're worrying me! What's the problem?"

"I...I...oh my God."

"Are you sick?"

"I...just don't know what happened to me. I was there. It was me. But it couldn't have been me..."

"What's going on? Should I call 911?" Steve started to get up.

"No..." Elise put a hand on his shoulder, "...silly. There is no need to panic...I guess. I think that I should be alone right now."

"You think?"

"I don't know anything right now."

"Let me rephrase that, but first Elise look at me!" Steve paused until their eyes met. "What do you want?

"I'm not sure if it's proper."

"Fuck proper! Elise, I love you, and you're scaring me! If I can help, I want to."

"I love you too. But there's nothing you can do."

"I can listen."

"But...I don't think it's right to tell you."

"If you don't want to tell me, then that's fine, but I'm not sure that's what you're telling me."

"It sounds perverse, but I want to tell you."

Steve waited.

"I have just had a...I guess you would call it a flashback. I was getting raped. It wasn't me, because I have never been raped. But it was me! I could see it. It's as if it was a movie. I was observing myself." Her voice had a ghost-like quality to it. "My distant past. How could I have forgotten? It was me."

An involuntary shudder shook her body.

"I have been raped."

* * *

A MISSION STATEMENT

To sit and judge people, day after day, one gets good at separating the weeds from the blossoms. To hear people's fears and dreams on a regular basis makes one a powerful sage. Fools, all of them, to think they are the only ones with problems, or that their problems are different. They are all the same. From child abuse issues, to just a general feeling of being unloved as a child, they are all trite excuses.

He was tired of hearing excuses.

Two simple words: "Grow up." How he longed to say them to so many different people.

Was he the only one who could see through all the bullshit?

Why was it up to him?

He placed his head in his hands. Too much burden for one man.

Too many...and too little time.

At one time he had enjoyed his work; at one time he had enjoyed his calling. But now he was fatigued.

He listened to problems; and he solved problems. Both were making him weary.

For him the future was set in stone. A prophecy of death.

At one time he laughed at psychics, but now he knew that he was one. Maybe the greatest psychic off all time!

After all, he could tell who was to die. And his only prediction was a general one—that the list was growing.

CHAPTER VI

DREAMS REALIZED

Where to Turn?

Things were going about as well as could be expected.

I still loved Elise. I also felt sorry for her. She was going through some real trying times stemming from her recent revelation.

I could only imagine her inner turmoil. I could sense her eagerness to love; yet she was so afraid. She had blocked out her rape and, until now, kept it successfully buried in her subconscious. We all want to fall in love, nothing can make me believe otherwise. Yet, sometimes the reality of the past keeps us from realizing that want. To express oneself in love both mentally and physically creates a vulnerability that can leave past pains and future fears totally exposed. I know that we all have remarkable resiliency as human beings, and that by blocking out, or forgetting, painful events we are using a protective mechanism that enables us to continue with everyday life. Continue but not flourish. To flourish we need to face and to cope. It would seem our subconscious buries horrible memories until a time we are ready to face them and get on with our lives.

So was Elise ready? I couldn't judge, but I trust in her inner being in relaying that it was time, by choosing now to uncover her buried memories.

She was a brave and wonderful person for choosing (even on a subconscious level) to face her past. It may sound strange, but my love for her has only been expanded by this realization.

She still loved me. She was also a little afraid, of me...of men...of life in general.

Her reality had come crashing down around her. Painful memories, long buried, were now coming up. At first she had been a mere observer, but each flashback went a little further, and was more frightening and real. She was ready to face these memories, I was sure of it, but she needed help.

Where could she turn?

Naturally I wanted her to turn to me, yet I knew that I could not be everything to her. She needed guidance in handling her new memories and the thoughts and emotions relating to them.

I turned her toward a man who had helped me through some pretty confusing times—Dr. Jack Rossintaul. I talked her into making an appointment with him.

He could help her. I was sure of it.

He was understanding and patient, after all, look how sympathetic he had been with me when I told him of my love for Elise and how I was afraid that she was leading me on.

Yes, Dr. Jack was the man for the job...

* * *

Since Elise's appointment with Dr. Jack was a week away I tried to be there for her as much as humanly possible. I gave her my pager number and told her there were no restrictions. We still went out twice that week, but it really wasn't much like any of our previous dates. I kissed her on the cheek at the end of them, and upon returning home I gave her a call to check on her.

It was a difficult week for me as well as her. I was treating her with kid gloves. I didn't want to say or do anything to upset her. It was making me weary.

Finally Friday rolled around, and with her appointment just a weekend away I think we were both feeling a little relief. But then I may have been wrong about her, because by the end of our date she detonated on me.

"I'm still the same person you fell in love with!"

"What's wrong?"

"You! You're treating me like I've got some sort of a terminal disease."

"I just..." I wasn't sure what to say.

"JUST SAY IT!"

"I don't want to upset you."

"Don't you see, the way you're treating me just makes things more confusing for me?"

"I'm just trying to be understanding."

"Maybe I shouldn't have told you." She looked away, trying not to cry.

"Elise...I'm sorry."

"Can't you be loving and understanding without being so saccharine?"

"I realize that this is new for you, but it's also new for me. I don't know how to act!"

"I fell in love with you. You! Why would I want you to change the way you act? I'm going through enough changes. With all my confusing thoughts and feelings, you're the one thing I can depend on. If you change, you're really going to send me over the edge."

"Just remember..." I smiled. "If you go, I'm coming too!"

"Maybe we could share a room at the asylum."

A shiver ran down my spine as I realized that "over the edge" had a whole different meaning to me.

* * *

It had been a tough week for me not just in my interactions with Elise, and finally getting put in my place by her, but something else was going on with me—nightmares. I knew they had to be related to the Elise remembrances, because they started they day after her revelation, but they never directly involved her.

I have a history of trying to decipher my dreams. It can be insightful, and I have, through experience, learned to trust my dreams. Especially the obvious ones that showed a clear path or direction.

But these dreams felt more like the confused nightmares of a small child. I'm not sure that I can take anything away from them, except, maybe, fear.

The first one was of me wandering. Presumably I was lost. I wasn't panicked in the dream. Even upon waking I thought very little of it. It just left me with a sort of archaic feeling. Everything was passing me by, and I didn't notice, or care.

Another dream had me on a game show. Some people were cheering, some were screaming obscenities, but most were just making noise. It was very chaotic. I was being asked by the host to make a decision. But I had no idea what I was supposed to do. "I have no decisions to make!" I keep telling him, but things didn't quiet down until I awoke. The buzzing of my alarm clock almost sounded peaceful.

Probably the most disturbing dream was of me being trapped in a small room. There were no doors and no windows. There was just a bed, and very little light. It seemed like forever I was trying to figure a way out, finally I just gave up and sat on the corner of the bed. I grew tired, and I lay back in the bed to rest. But there was someone there!

It was a naked woman. I looked but could not see her face. It didn't take me long to realize that I was also naked. She reached out to me, and I responded. Soon I was making love to this faceless woman.

The room faded. All there was in the world was this woman and I.

Even the bed disappeared from beneath us. It's as if we were floating in the blackness of empty space. All my focus was on her and our lovemaking. The direct physical world and the connection between this "mystery woman" and I were all that mattered. I was lost with no wish to be found. My awareness was locked only on the situation and my impending orgasm.

But vaguely I became aware of something else. Someone else. The woman. I looked at her again. Suddenly I realized that my thrusts were pushing her away. She was falling! She grabbed onto my penis and was hanging on. She looked up at me. It was Liz! I pulled back in shock and she lost her grip, and as she fell the voice that called out was Elise's. I reached for her in vain.

I watched her fall.

I woke up sobbing. Worse yet, I was sticky. It was the most horrible wet dream I could imagine.

I had some other crazy dreams that I only remember parts of and that generally I could make no sense of.

I told Elise nothing of my dreaming spree, for she had enough things going on herself. I tried to convince myself that these weird dreams were just my fears of being close to someone. For this was a new place for me. There was a depth of feeling here that I have never experienced. It was appropriate to be a little afraid.

But somehow I couldn't shake the feeling that there was something else wrong. Something I was missing, or overlooking, or...I wish I knew!

* * *

SUNDAY

Peaceful. That's how I awoke.

Slowly I opened my eyes. I looked at the time on my alarm clock. It said eight thirty. I was well rested; I had had a complete night of sleep without those crazy dreams haunting me like every other night. I lay there for about fifteen minutes listening to the glorious silence of a fresh new morning.

My thoughts drifted to Elise—quickly I glanced back at my alarm clock. It was Sunday. One day away from her appointment with Doctor Jack. I would like to see her. I smiled to think of her finally meeting Dr. Jack. I had talked about him so much to her, and now she was seeing him herself. I was sure he could help her. He was going to meet the woman of my dreams, I'm sure he would take that into consideration when he counseled her. The last he knew, she, the love of my life, was turning down my sexual advances. Wait until he found out about her excuse! Maybe he already figured it out, after all, he was a professional.

At least she had a reason to be screwed up, what was my excuse?

I laughed at the thought of him saying something like, "Steve's too screwed up for you. Stay away from him!" But my laugh felt awkward.

I lay there, trying to clear my head. Trying to hold onto that peaceful feeling that I awoke with. I tossed and turned, but could not outsmart the uncomfortable feeling that was growing in me.

Elise!

Hearing her voice would clear my head.

I grabbed the phone and my fingers effortlessly glided over the familiar numbers that would connect me with my love.

"Hello."

"Hi, Elise. I don't mean to bother you, but I was just wondering if you wanted to do something today?"

"I can't."

Silence fell between us, and finally I spoke up, "Why, you got a date?"

"Sort of..."

"Oh yea?" I teased.

"I really didn't want to tell you. I wanted to wait until it was over. He said it would be best not to tell anyone."

Suddenly I felt flush. I couldn't speak, thankfully—for then she said, "Dr. Rossintaul called not more than a half hour ago. Said he had an opening today. If I wanted."

"So you're going to see him today instead of Monday?"

"That's right. At ten o'clock."

"You sure you want to?"

"I want to get this over with."

I didn't have the heart to tell her that she would have to see him more than once. Therapy took time, sometimes years. Maybe she meant that she wanted to get this started, but somehow I doubted it. She did sound strange; I asked her if something was wrong.

"I'm pretty nervous."

"You're going to be fine."

"He told me not to tell anyone. He must be good, I think he could sense my jitters and he wanted to spare me any more pressure. I wasn't going to tell you..." her voice trailed off.

"Pressure? Nonsense! Remember, you're doing this for yourself. Not for anyone else—especially me. All you need from me is my love. And I want you to know that you will always have it."

"I don't usually get this nervous, but then again, two weeks ago I would have said that I have never been raped."

"I'll always be here for you."

"I know...I love you."

"I love you, too."

"So is this Dr. Jack really that good?"

"I liked him—he helped me. If you don't like him, don't worry about it, there are almost as many psychiatrists as there are lawyers!" I laughed.

"So if he screws me up, at least we can sue him!"

"Don't worry," I turned a bit more serious, "nothing's going to happen that you can't handle."

"Like if I find out I was fucked by a whole football team without my knowledge."

I choked back a laugh when I realized she was serious.

I wanted to offer to give her a ride to his office, but I didn't want to invade her space. Anyway I figured if she wanted a ride she could always ask.

I wanted to be there for her, I just didn't know how without seeming controlling.

"Babe," I revealed, "I'm trying to understand your pain, and God knows I know your fear. I wish I could have protected you from what happened to you. And I wish I could hold you safe in my arms forever, but sometimes these things are best getting out in the open. We can't change the fact of the things that have happened to us, we can only change the way we look at them today. Facing isn't always the easiest, but it's always the best."

"I guess I know that," she said. "I love you," and with that she hung up.

She gave me no time to respond. The sound of the dial tone droned in my ear. I hung up the phone, suddenly tired—no, weary. I rolled over and fell, almost instantly, into a restless sleep...

...Right into dreamland. This time it's not so much of a nightmare, it has sort of a surrealistic tranquility to it.

I am floating. I see Elise. I try to turn to follow her, but I have no control of my direction. I call out—but have no voice. The ultimate weightlessness.

So off I drift. As if on a cloud, I lay back and enjoy. I feel free, and can't even imagine offering resistance, for my present course poses no threat.

I look below to see Dr. Jack. He is reading a paper. He looks relaxed and has a smile on his face. He is far away and I strain to make out his features, although I am sure that it is him.

I try with minimal unsuccessful effort to steer myself down to him. He doesn't notice me as I drift past him overhead.

Again, I relax and enjoy the journey.

Before long, I see something up ahead. It is a man. Sitting. Reading a paper. Again it is Dr. Jack. He is a little closer now. I can see that it is definitely him. My attempt to stop is even more inconsequential than last time.

This time as I float by I try to read the paper he is holding. There are large headlines, yet I still am not close enough to make them out.

This process repeats several times, each of which I drift by a little closer until...I can read his paper. It looks familiar. It is my paper. The one from my car that I took to his office that one day. The one whose headlines screamed, "Murder! Again!"

There was also another object in the room. It was a finger painting. It looked like a Rorschach test, but instead of black it was done in red, and was signed Dr. Jack Rossintaul at the bottom.

The red paint was still all over his hands, and splotches of it were on the paper he was reading.

The nothingness of his surroundings soon melded into his office. He seemed comfortable, but there was a certain anticipation in the air, as if he were waiting for something.

With a loud, clear voice he said, "Next!"

It seemed his voice awoke me, I sat up with a smile on my face. Of course he was waiting—for his next patient!

Maybe it was Elise.

I took a deep breath, and couldn't let it out.

I gasped. I felt about to vomit. I ran to the bathroom.

Splashing water on my face, I looked into the eyes of a stranger in the mirror. They looked back at my accusingly.

I threw on some clothes and headed out the door. I glanced back at my clock on the way out and it read five minutes to ten.

The morning paper was on my steps as I rushed past, this time I didn't stop for it. I needed no more warnings. No more clues. My eyes were finally open. God, I hoped I was wrong. God, I hoped I was on time.

The twenty minute ride would be all in prayer.

* * *

DEATH BECOMES EWE

Steve's car raced, but could not keep up with his thoughts.

Why did it have to come to this?

Why had it taken so long for him to discern?

Please, please, please, please let it not be too late.

Did he have a secret wish to destroy everything around him? Or at least to stand by and watch his world crumble, while he just wrings his hands? Watching, waiting, expecting the next wall to crumble. Passively standing by, with barely enough energy and willpower to step aside while his world crashes at his feet.

He had a great effect on everyone's life, except his own. But the people around him affected him, and as each one crashed and burned, a little of him went too. And the one who had affected him the most was in grave danger.

He should have seen it coming. He should have known.

It was all his fault.

As he pulled into the parking lot, wheels screeching, he suddenly realized that the one he loved most in the world might not, at this moment, be in the world anymore.

With a lump in his throat he bounded out of his car and up the steps to the office. The sign on the front door said, "Dr. J. Rossintaul, M.D."

* * *

Steve pushed on the door. It was locked.

Dr. Rossintaul's office was closed today. The whole building was closed. The dates must have gotten mixed up!

With a sigh of relief, Steve realized that Elise's appointment must be next week. Today was Sunday; patients were never seen on Sunday. Either Elise must have heard wrong, or Steve must have misunderstood Elise. Smile on his face, he went back to his car.

He was about to get in his car when his eyes scanned the parking lot. His vision went blurry momentarily and he had to brace himself against his fender, for, not thirty feet away, was Elise's car.

Panic gripped him.

"Damn, why didn't I ever get a car phone!"

Steve scanned the area for a payphone, but none was within his vision. By the time he searched for a phone to call the police, it might be too late. He tried to block out the fact that it might already be too late out of his mind.

* * *

OFFICE VISIT

All was done, but to wait.

His office was clean, spotless. His adrenaline was already flowing, yet he sat behind his desk, trying to feint patience.

He got up from his desk, with a quick stride he was over to his bookshelf. He wiped the top of a few books. No dust here.

Where was she? Steve was always on time. But isn't that just like a woman? To be fashionably late. To be fashionably heartless.

He looked at his watch. Damn, it was only three past ten! He felt ready to explode. Only three minutes so far!? What would he do if she were fifteen minutes late? He couldn't stand to wait much longer. Maybe he should go out to meet her in the parking lot. The anticipation was killing him.

The anticipation of another patient.

The anticipation of a new patient.

The anticipation of meeting Steve's so-called flame.

The anticipation of the first mission encounter in his office.

The anticipation of doing something to relieve the large feeling that was uncomfortable in his tight dress pants. He wondered if Elise was good-looking.

The anticipation of her possibly being his first interview victim. For in the beginning he had planned that he would interview these evil women before punishing them, but somehow it had not worked out that way. How fitting that she was the first! He knew of her guilt, for he trusted Stephen, and Stephen had explained her guilt to him. Poor Stephen didn't even know what an evil creature she was. Leave it to Dr. Rossintaul. The doctor would clean up the mess. Wipe up the dirt spot in Steve's life. More filth to be wiped off the planet. All in a day's work...

He paced his office. His imagination ran wild. He pictured how he would get through to her. He could see her blood on his hands. He could taste the scent in the air, her perfume mixed with fear; his sweat, his yearning. He knew he would have to take her. More than the killing he envisioned the sex. Would she pretend fear and pain, like the rest, or would she participate in her greatest act before her death? He knew he would use more force with her in sex, than in the actual killing of her. He was finally able to realize that the real power of his lessons came, not from the killing, but from the sex.

He thought of letting her live, for Steve's sake. But he knew that it was for Steve that he had to make sure he put an end to Elise's life. For Steve's love for her would probably only grow, setting himself up to be hurt more by her. She would recover, women were strong, but Steve would be entrapped forever in her hold. For Steve was a true innocent, as were most men, but Steve's naiveté was even deeper than most. Steve was a hopeless romantic, always looking for the bright side, even when none existed. Steve had trouble rising after each fall, never fully comprehending that it was all a game. So the one who had Steve's heart wrapped securely on a string could not be left to escape to continue to torment him and, when she was through with him, some other unsuspecting man.

Jack knew that he was different than almost all men, in that he could see through the wicked lies of the female gender. Thus was the mission set so firmly in his lap. Who else could carry on if he should stop?

Jack had started to grow weary from his missions, but now he felt a rejuvenation of spirit. Maybe it was from the fact that this was the first person he knew, the rest of the victims had been total strangers. Not that he really knew Elise. He had never met, or even seen Elise, but somehow he felt that he knew her, however slightly, through Steve. He didn't know what she looked like, how she carried herself, her voice, her choice of dress, or any of her mannerisms. Yet he knew her, knew her soul. It was not so much from what Steve had said about her, but more from his awkward silence, his frustrated pauses, and his tears...

It was enough for Jack to know her, and discern that she was just like the rest. They were all so similar that it made him shudder. And it wasn't that it was all females, otherwise he might as well indiscriminately kill each and every one he encountered. Some females were okay. Just as some males weren't. In his killing spree he had killed two males. He saw no significance that they were both obviously gay.

No, he had not had sex with either man. Although both were killed before he had started that particular inclination toward sex in his missions.

He firmly believed that it had nothing to do with genes, but that females were more often bred to be snobbish and cruel. The kind of stuff that he was weeding out was all learned behavior, which is what made it so bad, necessitating its removal.

"Upbringing," he sighed. It made him sad, for it seemed that they shouldn't let just anyone become parents. Parenting courses should be a requirement.

His thoughts drifted to his own childhood. His dad. His mom. They had loved him. They had brought him up right, hadn't they? So why did he hate them so? He shook away the memories. The quiver left him cold.

He heard a noise. He looked to his clock. Seven minutes late.

He hurried to his desk, but did not sit down. The little bell rang in his waiting room announcing the arrival of the next victim.

He took a few deep breaths and proudly noted his erection had gone down. He smoothed out his pants and opened up the door.

He greeted her and let her in. She was cute, in a deceiving way. For there was no way he could guess from appearance alone that this woman could be so wicked. But that made it all the worse. Hatred burned in him, attempting to rise up, but he subdued it the best he could by telling himself, "In a few minutes. In a few minutes." And he could feel his pants between his legs getting tight again.

"Have a seat, I'll be right back," he told her as he exited the door she had come in, being careful to keep his back to her.

He closed the door softly, then in a trot he ran down the flight of stairs to the outside door. He looked at the parking lot, where he saw only his car and one other. It must be hers. Good. That was the nice thing about Sunday, it seemed no one else worked. But to those with a mission, their work knew no rest.

He got into his car and pulled it around to the back of the building where it would be less conspicuous. He would worry about her car later, for soon enough he would have the keys to it.

Before he headed back he gave one more quick glance around, to make sure no one was watching. As he reentered through the glass doors he locked them behind him.

He bounded up the stairs two at a time, and when he was back in his office he was breathing hard and his heart was racing. "The best feeling in the world," he said to himself. He tried to contain his smile as he went back in to see Elise.

* * *

"Tell me about yourself," Doctor Jack suggested.

Elise talked about the town she grew up in. About her upbringing. About her life, in general terms.

"Tell me about what you want," he inquired.

She talked vaguely about dreams and goals.

"More specifically," he asked when she finally took a breath, "what do you want from therapy?"

Basically, a "successful relationship" was what she was trying to say behind her droning words.

He tuned out her words and concentrated more on her physical appearance. He could see she was nervous, but there was something more, maybe it was not in what she said but in the tone of her voice. Her words were careful, measured. When she said what she felt was a key word or phrase, she always looked up. Was she gauging his reaction? Was she scrutinizing his behavior? Was she sitting in judgement over him as a psychiatrist, or a man? Who did she think she was?

He had done a good job of hiding his disdain for the damn bitch, but it was getting more difficult the more he saw of her.

He watched her hands as they looked for a place to rest, but each time he thought they would finally be still, they nervously fluttered to a new position. Her feet were no better, except that they seemed to keep a more consistent rhythm. Back and forth. Shift right, then left. "One and two, one and two." It seemed he could almost keep time to her deranged feet.

He observed her breasts as they rose with each breath. They didn't seem too big, although it almost looked as if a bra was restraining them. Hey, nowadays bras were made to enhance and direct attention. Who was she trying to fool? Would the simple-minded psychiatrist be duped into thinking she was virtuous?

God, all her babbling was driving him crazy!

He tried to focus on her legs, but she just kept talking!

He knew there was only one way to make her shut up...

He got to his feet.

She watched him as he approached her. She sat up a bit straighter as he got within two feet. He could smell her perfume.

He crouched down next to her.

She stopped talking.

"Finally!" he thought. But when he looked into her eyes, he still saw the evilness within.

"Yes," he thought, "lure the pour defenseless fly into your trap."

But he was no ordinary fly. He longed to see the expression in her eyes when she realized this fact.

"What do you really want?" he asked, his voice cracked, as it seemed like hours since he last spoke.

"I don't understand," she said nervously.

He wondered how she would react if he placed his hand on her leg.

Would she scream? Probably just back away and act indignant, never letting on that she liked it.

This one was a tough cookie, with the heart of a predator. She was going to be a tough one.

He knew he needed to stay on top of the situation at all times. With his hands he tapped a little drum role on his knees, and when he saw her eyes divert to his knees he quickly glanced around the room to note any of her possible escape routes, and any potential weapons.

When he looked back at her she was still looking at his hands. But there was a look of...of...was that terror he saw in her eyes?

How could she know? Then he studied more closely the direction of her eyes and saw that she wasn't looking at his hands, but in-between them, to the bulge in his pants, for he was quite obviously hard.

He quickly rose and turned his back on her, and knowing he must diffuse the situation as quickly as possible he said, "I think that's enough for today."

"Yes," he heard her say, though it was barely a whisper.

"Yes," he repeated. "I'm not feeling myself today." He mumbled some stuff about a wife and leaving and aloneness, hoping she would fill in some blanks and bring about an assumption that he was just a troubled man and really meant no harm. He tried to sound vulnerable and afraid, and mostly, weak.

But Elise, noticing his sweat and heavy breathing since when he first came back into the office, had her guard up as she ignored his present mutterings and headed for the door.

She had it opened before he realized she was not behind him any longer.

"Elise," he said, almost in a shout.

"Yes?" she said as she turned back to look at him, holding the door halfway open.

Their eyes met. His eyes were the eyes of a puppy dog as he said, "Never mind," and fought off a sob. He secretly, silently, congratulated himself for a fine acting job.

But the instant he said, "Never mind," she continued out the door.

But with a flash he was also at the door.

Elsie tried to pull the door closed as quick as she could, but she wasn't quite fast enough. With a fury, his hand shot forth and caught the door before it was completely shut. She tugged on the door, trying to get it to close, not caring if it smashed his hand. But he was strong, and slowly he pulled the door open.

Then with total recklessness she threw her body against the door pushing it open and into him. He went tumbling back to the floor. She stumbled but kept her balance and with an agile pivot she was through the waiting room and into the hallway.

But he was like a cat. She never even heard him get back on his feet, but as she tried to run down the hall, a hand gripped her shoulder. It felt as though her shoulder would explode as that one strong hand brought her to her knees.

From the moment she walked into the office she had felt uncomfortable, but now for the first time the seriousness of the situation had fully come to her attention as she let out an ear-piercing scream.

It was about at that time that a car squealed its tires as it roared into the parking lot.

The two figures that fought in the empty office building had no hope of hearing the squealing tires, nor did anyone have a possibility of hearing a scream from outside the building.

* * *

Steve opened his trunk. Beneath the spare tire he grabbed out the tire iron. He was doing very little thinking at this point. Thinking of possibilities would only paralyze him.

He ran up to the glass doors and without thought or regret he brought it down upon the glass. The glass chipped. He looked on in disappointment. He had barely made a dent.

Repeatedly he brought the tire iron down on the glass, until he felt his arm would fall off. His head spun as he saw what little damage he was doing. He would never get in the building this way.

* * *

Darkness, like a drop of blood, coagulates on the soul. It starts off small, but it hardens and eats away all in its grasp. It doesn't so much grow as it consumes all else. It starts off simple, maybe as anger. Then it mutates and sneaks its slimy tendrils into other areas such as hate, violence, fury, and even murder. Each step further into depravity is still eventually not enough.

* * *

AFFAIR FIGHT

This one fought. Jack cursed himself for his sloppiness. This should have been his most triumphant mission but it was turning into a nightmare. She had succeeded in getting out into the hall, and he had tried to drag her back in before the real action started. But she had managed to dig her fingernails into his arms and hands, causing them to bleed, and now there might be signs of blood in the hallway—his blood!

Damn her!

He presently had her under control. In his waiting room. Door closed. She was face down on the ground with him on top of her. Both of his hands pinned her face to the ground. He knelt on each arm as he straddled her. She alternated great bursts of energy with moments of stillness as if she was trying to catch him off guard, more probably she was merely recuperating during the silent times. She had almost succeeded to throw him off several times summonsing up seemingly boundless energy.

Fuck her!

"Don't mind if I do," he thought, but his smile showed little gratification. It seemed a monumental task, for up to this point he hadn't even gotten her clothes off.

"You're more work than you're worth, bitch!" he told her.

She tried to say something but he pushed her face into the ground even harder, muffling any potential words. She had talked enough, one more word from her and he would snap her neck right here.

But her lesson wasn't over yet! Somewhere the lessons had

changed from mere death to rape. Of course death always followed the "sex." Death always had the final say.

"Sex, rape, what's the difference when you're dealing with a slut?" he thought.

He was starting to think instead of react and she made him aware of it by throwing him off her with one great push of her buttock. He went tumbling back. She was up in a flash.

But she didn't run.

Instead...she attacked.

It was almost as if it was in slow motion.

He watched in disbelief as she charged him. He was just struggling to his feet. He saw her coming. Saw her foot rise up.

He realized a platform shoe was coming hard at his groin.

About a foot from its target he managed to bring both of his hands up and with them he pushed her leg up before it hit its intended target. She flipped up in the air and landed on the back of her head with a thud. Her solid heal had missed his groin but when he pushed it up and away, from the shear momentum of her kick, it still came forward and caught the front of his face. It scraped and dug through the soft flesh there as his nose felt like it was getting pushed up to his forehead.

He tried to recover quickly, but momentarily lost hold of his bearings as he gasped for breath with blood filling his nostrils and also speckling his vision.

He wiped a hand across his face to find that he was bleeding profusely.

But he had no time to lick his wounds, she was probably down the stairwell by now.

With his sleeve he wiped off as much of the blood as he could, clearing his vision as best he could.

He took one step forward, as he prepared himself for a sprint. Bloody face or not, he was determined that there was no way she was going to outrun him.

He stepped on something.

Sprawled out.

On the floor.

She hadn't gone anywhere.

He carefully knelt down next to her. Was she faking? Dead? Unconscious? Or just dazed?

She must have hit her head. His hand to her chest told him she was not dead, for he felt movement there.

Her eyes were open.

She was making a sound. More of a low moan.

She wasn't dead, yet, or even unconscious. "Good," he said.

Grabbing her feet, he dragged her into his office, where he could do things right.

* * *

CONFLICTING OPINIONS

Steve pounded on, kicked, and threw his body full force into the glass. It chipped, it even cracked, but it would not break. Tears mixed with sweat, streamed down his face. He was exhausted, out of breath, sore, his hands were bleeding and throughout it all he cursed himself.

It was his fault.

The woman he loved was probably dead, and he played games out here.

He was clearly to blame, and it didn't help to play "what ifs" all day long. If he was correct, he would play "what ifs" for the rest of his life.

He felt helpless and hopeless.

He could not get in. He should have went for the police, they would have been here by now. Maybe he still should go.

He headed to his car at a run. His thoughts ran faster now than his legs ever could. If the glass door hadn't been up seven cement steps at the entrance he would have rammed his car into the building. It sounded crazy, but he would have done it! If he was wrong, oh well!

He would take the chances of a big fine, arrest and jail time. He could be wrong about his suspicions, but what if he was right?

Maybe he was paranoid, but too much added up.

He had even tried the back door, but his fists and a metal crowbar weren't going to make a dent there—it was steal!

As he revved up his car and threw it into reverse he had a thought. It was crazy, but at this point there wasn't much sanity left in the world.

He spun the car around to the back of the building and...there were no steps!

Yes, the door was small and steal, but if he could get his car going fast enough and he hit it just right, maybe he could dent it in just enough to gain access to the building.

With no hesitation he pulled his car to within fifty feet of the back door and floored it.

* * *

First thing's first. Jack headed to the bathroom to clean himself up. Elise was on his couch, she wasn't going anywhere. But was he sure about that? He had been wrong before. He did not want to underestimate her again.

He stopped a few feet from the bathroom, looking back at her. He could still feel blood trickling down his face and neck. He had to at least stop the bleeding. He decided he would do minimal repair to himself until she was taken care of. He knew he had all day to clean up better, for it was Sunday.

He also was in dire need of some aspirin to halt the throbbing in his head.

Cold water stung his face, as he watched the sink turn red. Upon inspection his cuts weren't as bad as he thought. A few well-placed Band-Aids took care of almost all the bleeding. There had been an awful lot of blood for the few cuts he had. He worked gingerly around his nose, for it was very sore. He didn't think it was broken, but that didn't stop it from hurting like a son-of-a-bitch.

It took him less than ten minutes to clean himself up, but don't think that he didn't peek out at Elise every chance he could. He was getting very cynical in his maturity.

She was conscious when he came out, but was acting as if she had been drugged.

Jack sat her up on the couch and then sat next to her.

She looked at him with blank eyes.

He reached over and began unbuttoning her blouse.

It looked like she was trying to focus as she asked, "Is this real?"

He smoothly removed her shirt and smiled, "This is the only real thing in your life. All else has been a lie."

His fingers deftly unbuckled her pants, and they were off before her slow motion brain could have another thought.

He looked at her asking, "Aren't you even going to fight?" He couldn't help thinking about the still and quiet one who got this whole sex-craving thing started for him. Anger rose in him.

She took so long to answer, he assumed she hadn't heard him when she said, "I should. I know that."

"Is this a test?" Elise vaguely recalled why she was here, something about remembering an event a lot like this one. Why had she chosen to remember? She was well aware that her thought process was faulty, she was just trying to hold on to consciousness and to somehow keep from going insane.

Maybe this was all an illusion.

Or maybe everything else was an illusion, and that she had never left that rape of years ago. It made sense, because she felt like she was stuck. Her head was in a fog and her vision blurry. The whole world pressed down on her and she could not move.

Her slow moving brain knew enough that it didn't want to be here. She had to get away, and since it was clear that escaping physically had been impossible, she knew her only other option was to mentally go away.

He reached around her to undo her bra, and noticed blood, mostly dried, on her back. There was a trail from her head. But not much. Hell, he had washed more blood down the sink. More of his blood had been shed than hers. He would rectify that soon enough.

"But first thing's first!" A forceful hand reached up and grabbed her panties and violently ripped them down to her ankles.

She moved a slow hand up, as if to protest, but with his free hand he knocked it back so hard that he was sure he also bruised his own hand.

Then he removed his own clothes.

Then there was a crash.

"What the Hell?" he had immediate thoughts of an earthquake as the whole building shook.

Then it shook again.

* * *

The airbag was in his face.

Steve opened his door and ran around to the front of the car. The door to the building was definitely dented, and so was his car. He tried to push the steel door open, but it wouldn't budge, and it wasn't bent enough for him to squeeze through.

Without further thought, he was back in his car. It didn't want to move, as the fender was bent back into the tire, but with enough gas it lurched back as rubber fumes filled the air.

This time he angled the collision so that it would take place on the driver's side corner, as the passenger side was twisted and bent metal that wouldn't serve his purpose.

Again, he floored it. Before he hit the door there was a pop as the passenger side tire blew, but that didn't stop his forward momentum as the left corner of his car caught the door perfectly again, and this time it flew away in one piece.

Steve wasn't able to watch this event though, because as the car hit the building his body slammed into the steering wheel, and the windshield also exploded.

He had little squares of glass all over him and his chest was feeling some discomfort, but he was out the door and into the building before he could think of his own pain.

* * *

NICE MEETING YOU HERE

Steve knew that he was an unexpected guest but that, with the noise of his entry, Dr. Jack would be prepared.

With the advantage of total surprise gone, he sent the elevator up to the second floor, then ran up the stairs.

But he didn't come bounding out the second floor landing, he waited. Only when he heard the "ding" of the elevator did her peer around the corner. He saw a man down by the elevator, keeping close to the wall, waiting to surprise the passenger. It was Dr. Jack. Steve's heart almost stopped when he realized that he was not wearing a shirt.

Trying to suppress any subsequent thoughts, he quietly slipped across the hall and into Dr. Jack's office.

Steve quietly closed the door behind him. "Elise," his voice no more than a whisper, "Elise, are you here?"

He was still out of breath from the run up the stairs, yet he tried not to take too deep of breaths because his chest hurt from the crash. "Elise!" he called out a bit louder as he went into Dr. Jack's office.

She wasn't there.

At least not alive.

Sure, if she was dead, she could be stuffed underneath the desk or couch or anywhere. If she was dead then nothing mattered. If she was dead then his dominant thought would be of joining her. How could he live without the light that had finally come into his life?

He didn't want to find the body, but he knew that he must. Filled with dread, he looked under places no live body could fit like someone searches for rattlesnakes in their bed. He knew he had to hurry before Dr. Jack returned, but he felt like he was in a slow motion movie. He had no motivation to find Elise's cold lifeless body, other than by doing it quickly he might get out before Dr. Jack comes back and thus save his own miserable skin. But what was the point if Elise was dead?

He heard a noise.

Dr. Jack returning. Choices ran through his brain—fight, flight, or surrender.

Every muscle in his body tensed up, and he knew what he would do. He would kill that dog and make him feel the pain of each one of his victims.

There was a small thought inside his head that questioned his sanity in thinking that Dr. Jack could be a murderer. But somehow he knew, to the core of his being, that this all added up to only one conclusion, that Dr. Jack was the murderer from the paper that day. That Steve had put his faith and trust in a man who was completely mad. And worse yet, he had sent the love of his life to this madman, to be tortured and murdered.

With a furor, Steve turned toward the noise. But it wasn't coming from the outside door, but from another closed door. He approached slowly, cautiously, and opened up the bathroom door...

He rushed forward to take Elise into his arms.

In that fraction of a second it took for him to get to her, some things registered with him—

She was totally naked.

She didn't rush toward him.

She looked like a deer caught in headlights.

And that...*she was alive*!

He took her into his arms.

"You're so cold!" he told her.

"Steve!" she said as if she was guessing. Her speech was slightly slurred.

"What did he do to you?" he hugged her tight to his chest.

"Who?" she questioned as if she had no idea what was going on.

"You are still in danger. We have to get out of here. Where are your clothes?" He was talking fast, and when he saw that she really didn't follow what he asked he said, "Never mind! Let's just go."

He took her hand and started for the door, but she pulled her hand back.

Trying to talk gently, but aware that some urgency was still in his voice he said, "We must leave now."

When she made no response he started to pick her up but she spoke up, "No, I will follow you." And she placed her hand in his.

He pulled off his shirt and put it around her, and they headed out the door together.

* * *

Out the door, into the hall, down the hallway, to the stairs, down the stairs, and out to his car. They made it safely.

When Steve saw his car he realized the mistake he had made, he mouthed three small words, "Oh my God." It was undriveable.

Elise, she had her car here too!

But she obviously wasn't carrying her keys.

He didn't know what to do. He didn't feel safe leaving her here alone while he went back up to look for her keys, but if he took her with him it would slow him down. They were lucky to avoid Dr. Jack up until this point, but going back up into his office was only asking for disaster.

Then came a sound that was music to his ears. In the distance he heard a siren. And as he listened for a moment he could tell it was growing closer.

"We'll just wait," he told Elise, even though he wasn't sure she could comprehend much of anything right now. "The police are coming."

Steve looked at the woman he loved and spoke softly, "You're safe now. You're going to be okay."

She had to be okay. He had noticed the blood on her, but only now had time to look at the bump on the back of her head.

"Ow!" she said when he touched it.

"You will be okay," he repeated, more for his benefit than hers.

"I'm okay, you're okay," came a voice from the top of the stairs, "her—I'm not too sure about!"

"Jack!" Steve spit out the name. His first instinct was to rush

Jack and pummel him into senselessness. Then in an instant he thought of Elise, and stepped in front of her in a protective manner. His next thought was to flee; he took Elise's hand and looked to the door.

All these thoughts happened in approximately five seconds and were canceled out by the vision of the gun in Jack's hand.

"Don't move," Jack confirmed the situation.

Bounding down two steps at a time, Jack was close enough to pollute their air. "Now, you move!" He waved the gun at Jack.

"I'm not going anywhere without her!"

Jack laughed.

Trying to control his rage, Steve took a deep breath and winced in agony as a stabbing pain in his chest told him it was not time to be macho.

"Just like your little girlfriend, I don't think you're one hundred percent. Still, you better move quickly..."

"No!"

"Oh, yes, and you can bring her too."

"She can't go anywhere in this state. Leave her here, take me."

"Actually, I would like to leave you. But you went and fucked it all up." He cocked the gun and aimed it at Elise. "Hell, I could just kill her here."

"We'll go!" Steve pulled Elise through the door with him. "But my car is toast, and we're not going to get to far on foot with her in this condition."

"Remember she drove too!" Jack said in a mocking tone.

"I don't think she's carrying her keys on her..." Steve's voice trailed off as Jack dangled the keys, and the flipped them to Steve. "You drive," he said.

They made it across the parking lot to her car. The sirens were getting louder.

"Hurry up!"

The blue Accord pulled out of the parking lot with Steve at the wheel and Elise in the front seat next to him. Jack was in the back seat, his gun alternating between the back of each of their heads.

Within a minute of their departure, a police car, sirens blaring, roared into the parking lot.

* * *

"Why?" was all that Steve could think to say.

"Shut up and drive. Don't try to psychoanalyze me!"

Jack looked around the car—a little dirty, but fairly neat. He was surprised. He had expected her to be a slob. Sometimes looks were deceiving...

The rest of the drive was in silence. Each man was trying to think. Each man wanted a way out.

They were back at Elise's place. Jack reasoned that they couldn't go to either of the men's places because the police might come looking for them. After all, it was Steve's car smashed at the back door, and it was Jack's office that showed signs of a struggle. But there was nothing to suggest Elise's involvement. Jack had never entered her name in his appointment book, and he never even took her name or address for billing information. According to all records, she was not one of Dr. Jack's patients and had never been.

Jack felt that he owed Steve something, after all, he was killing Elise for Steve's benefit, although he would never understand that. But now they both had to die, Elise for being evil and Steve for being stupid. "Do you want to see how it works?" he asked Steve.

"You are killing innocent people!"

"In your naivete, you see them as innocent. I see through their guises," Jack explained.

"You see! You see! You see nothing but your pain!" Steve spat.

"Do I look to be in pain?" Jack calmly smiled.

"Your pain is in your actions, not in your appearance." Steve fought to control his temper. He wanted to be able to think rationally, and be able to take advantage of any opportunities.

"On the contrary, I see your pain."

"What!?"

"I see you, and others like you who let these scum," he made a gesture towards Elise, "tear you up."

"So you tear them up!" Steve had thoughts of knocking some sense into the "bad" doctor.

"Eye for an eye sort of thing." Jack smiled.

Steve was attempting to win a shouting match that Jack wasn't going to participate in. Steve knew he had to play Jack's game. He said in as even a voice as he could manage, "We make a vengeful God to cover our own vengeance in our hearts."

"So says the Bible."

"Written by man, with his owns fears and fallacies."

"Inspired by God!" thundered Jack.

"A dog's interpretation of a great poem will only be angry barks."

"God created man! Therefore if man is flawed, then so is God!"

"God is our father. He can only hope his children fulfill their destiny."

"Then why did he make them so evil!?"

"Not evil. You, of all people, should know that they need understanding."

"Impossible! They are evil!" Jack stood up, turning his back on Steve.

Steve got ready to rise from his seat and make a rush, but the distance made him think better of it.

"Maybe it is impossible here and now, but in time..." Steve rationalized.

"A lifetime! I've spent my life trying to understand!"

"The first step in understanding is acceptance."

"I can't accept it! No one should have to!" Jack went from screaming to a moderate, contemplating state. He sat down and said, "It's not right. It's so unfair to feed on the defenseless. They don't know what it's like when you trust them and put all your faith in them."

"Do you still sometimes feel defenseless?" Steve asked, trying to keep the incredulity out of his voice.

"No! Not me!" Jack was back on his feet, waving the gun around, voice raised, "Not anymore!"

"So now you know!"

"I'm one of the only ones!"

"So you can't be hurt any more."

"No!"

"You've learned."

"But now that I know, I've got to help others!"

"How is killing helping?"

"They can't hurt anyone again."

"But they do continue to hurt," Steve realized.

"No! They are dead, all of them. They will not hurt anyone again," Jack exulted.

Steve just nodded his head.

"Who!? Who could they possible hurt!?

"You."

A pained expression flashed across Jack's face.

Steve went on, "You say that you see my pain, well, let me tell you that I see your pain, too." Steve closed his eyes and rubbed his temples with his fingertips. "Maybe that is why I trusted you. To open up my heart. To expose my weaknesses. I saw your pain. And I knew that my own pain could be, if not understood, then, at least, accepted."

Steve swallowed. "I see...feel...your pain. It has been growing. Now I see why. With each victim. With each death. Like a burden."

"Each death frees me. The burden is that there are so many. So many more..."

"No, you dread the so many more because you know it is wrong." The sorrow in Steve's voice was only surpassed by its conviction.

"It is my mission!"

"Your mission is to figure it out. The problem will always remain."

"No! I just need to be more patient!" It was Jack's turn to close his eyes.

Steve waited for Jack to open them again before he said, "It is like the schoolboy, who is called to the front of the class to work his first division problem. In a fit of frustration he breaks the blackboard, and exults, "There! Problem solved!" Steve looked deep into Jacks eyes, "Your killing has solved nothing."

"In the large scheme of things, maybe not. But still, with each one gone, there is one less to hurt others."

"How about you?" Steve repeated.

"I am...sacrificing myself. I accept damnation for the betterment, and protection of others."

"How about you?"

"I am the judge."

"And who judged you?"

"No one judges me now!"

"Who judged you?"

"No one will again!"

"When was it?"

"It was so long ago. Forgotten."

"Who judged you?"

"Mom! My goddamn mother, okay!?"

"And your father?" questioned Steve.

"He turned the key. On the closet door. He tied the ropes. He preformed the tests." Jacks body was shaking in convulsions. "Mom never laid a hand on me. She just rated the torture. I hated her the most. I don't think he would have done any of it, if not for her judging. Nodding her approval."

Looking up, a sad smile quivered on his lips. "It was Mom who was the evil one." He said it with a new found conviction, "Dad was just a victim...merely another victim."

Tears started to flow. "I was just a little boy...I was just a little boy. I didn't know any better. I think I still loved them...for years!"

"But now you do know better. What they did was wrong. Blame them now! Call them evil! Stop blaming yourself. And stop blaming other hurt souls like yourself. They are not evil. Just afraid. And withdrawn."

Jack broke down, his gun dropped to the floor. Jack fell to his knees sobbing. Jack was vulnerable; Steve had his opportunity to overtake him.

Steve picked up the gun.

He put it in his pocket.

Bending down to Jack's level, he extended his arm and wrapped it around Jack.

Jack cried for the terrible pain he felt inside. Steve cried too, for the needless death of so many innocent people.

After a few moments Steve got up and went over to the phone. He dialed "911," then went to Elise, who was sleeping in the next room.

"Everything will be all right," he promised.

He kissed her, then pulling a cover up around her shoulders, he said a short prayer for her.

He went back to Jack and sat next to him, waiting for the police to arrive.

* * *

STEVE'S LAST WORDS

A voice, clear, loud—yet only inside my head. A voice like none I have ever witnessed, "Go forth my son, and bring light to the world."

I fell upon my knees. Sobs welled up from within. Tears came out to cleanse.

Burying my face in my hands, I knew myself not to be worthy.

Looking up to no place in particular, I cried out in a forceful voice, that astonished even me, "Is it I?"

I repeated it over and over again, but no answer came.

I went to bed with awe as my foundation. Could it possibly be true? Was I, who felt totally human, vulnerable, and with all the same fears and shortcomings as everyone else, possibly the Son?

Of God?

I prayed that night until sleep came over me, like a quiet tide that rose up and around me, carrying me off.

A dream. I was at a table. It was dinnertime. A grand figure came into the room and sat at the head of the table. He was almost too bright to look at, yet, somehow pleasing to the eye.

I felt good just to be in the same room with this figure. I felt blessed.

"Hello, son," was all that he said to me, yet the knowledge set me free.

I looked to my hands, but saw no wounds upon my wrists.

Someone approached me from behind. I stood to acknowledge him. Turning to see that familiar face, to look into those loving eyes, I was speechless. He embraced me.

"Brother," was all he said, but I could feel the warmth and love of a million hearts.

"Jesus!" I exclaimed, and hugged him all the tighter.

We sat down together at the table.

A voice came from the head of the table, resounding, lucid, and very pleasing to the ear, "Let us pray my sons..."

At the completion of the prayer I heard a billion amens in unison, and I turned to, for the first time, really see the table that me, my brother, and father were sitting at. It was a table of humanity. All races, all religions. Everyone was there.

I awoke peaceful. I wanted to go back to my dream, yet I knew that I must go forth. It was time to meet and share with the rest of my family. The knowledge of a reunion would keep me focused. When one day, we could all take our proper place with our father in heaven, and at last, really be together as a family.

For he is the father to all. We, each and every one of us, are all his children, special, unique, yet blessed with the same strong love, if we can but learn the truth. The truth of love, and the truth of forgiveness. It will set us free.

Who better to learn the words of The Father from than his Son? Me.

This is the end.